COYOTE PETERSON

L B

...wn and Company

...York Boston

Citations

Chapter 2—Leeches

57   "Instead, they have three ridged, bladelike jaws with one hundred little razor-sharp, pointed teeth on each. When the leech opens its mouth, the jaws emerge like the petals of a blooming flower, looking like the letter Y when they are ready to sink into the host.": Shah, Richa. Hirudinaria: Habitat, Locomotion and Development. Biology Discussion. Oct. 3rd, 2019. Section 5. Fig 67.7

65   "The hirudin compound produced by the leeches can stay active in tissue for twelve to twenty-four hours in a laboratory setting. This, unfortunately, was not a laboratory setting. I knew I'd be bleeding into the next day.": Munro, R & Hechtel, F.O.P. & Sawyer, Roy. Sustained Bleeding after a leech bite in the Apparent Absence of Hirudin. Thrombosis and Haemostasis. July 1989

İkizceli İ, Avşaroğulları L, Sözüer E, et al. Bleeding due to a medicinal leech bite. Emergency Medicine Journal 2005; 22:458–460.

69   Family Matters (all content): Roth, M. The Biology of Leeches. Musculoskeletal Key. Oct. 3, 2016. https://musculoskeletalkey.com/the-biology-of-leeches/: Fig 3.2 Description under Anatomy and Function

Chapter 3—Canine

76   "According to the National Pet Owners Survey, forty-eight percent of households in the United States have at least one dog, resulting in a national dog population of about seventy-seven million and counting!": Brulliard, Karin & Clement, Scott. How Many Americans Have Pets? An Investigation of fuzzy statistics. The Washington Post. Jan. 31, 2019.

77   "According to the Centers for Disease Control and Prevention (CDC) approximately 4.7 million dog bites occur every year in the United States.": Gilchrist, J & Gotsch, K & Annest, JL & Ryan, G. Nonfatal Dog Bite—Related Injuries Treated in Hospital Emergency Departments—United States,

2001. Centers for Disease Control. July 4, 2003. https://www.cdc.gov/mmwr/preview/mmwrhtml/mm5226a1.htm

78   "Humans have had a long history with dogs creating close ties over thousands of years.": Morey, Darcy F. Dogs Domestication and the Development of Social Bond. (New York: Cambridge University Press, 2010) 24–37.

81   Fact blurb about Schutzhund: Jason Kerr, phone interview with author, October 13, 2019.

89   "Kevlar is a well-known material often used in protective armor such as ballistic vests, combat helmets, and firefighting suits.": Dupont. Kevlar Technical Guide. Dupont. 2017. https://www.dupont.com/content/dam/dupont/amer/us/en/safety/public/documents/en/Kevlar_Technical_Guide_0319.pdf

93, 95, 96, 100   All command translations: Jason Kerr, phone interview with author, October 13, 2019.

Chapter 5—Lobster

139   "Just like crabs and crayfish, lobsters have gills and breathe underwater." Kinckle, Sabrina. Lobsters and Gills. How do Lobsters Get Oxygen? PetsOnMom.com. September 26, 2017. https://animals.mom.me/how-do-lobsters-get-oxygen-12169360.html

142   "A female lobster tail is larger than a male's because they must have room to carry eggs. A one-pound female lobster can carry up to eight-thousand eggs, while a nine-pound female can carry up to one hundred thousand!": Pelletier, Antonina. Lobster 101: Reproduction and Life Cycle. Maine Lobster Community Alliance. October 19, 2019. https://mlcalliance.org/all-about-lobster/lobster-101-reproduction-and-life-cycle/

Chapter 6—Tokay

168   "Florida houses around 50 species of non-native reptiles, more than anywhere else in the world!": Florida Fish and Wildlife. Nonnative Reptiles, Florida's Nonnative Fish and Wildlife. Florida Fish and Wildlife. 1999–2019. https://myfwc.com/wildlifehabitats/nonnatives/reptiles/. September 2019.

Disclaimer: Coyote Peterson and the crew are professionally trained and receive assistance from animal experts when in potentially life-threatening situations. Never approach or attempt to handle wildlife on your own.

Contents

LET THE BITES BEGIN!

Here we go again...Coyote facing a world of pain!

What's going on, Coyote Pack, and welcome to my newest book, *The Beast of Bites*. It seems like a lifetime ago that I willingly placed my arm into the mouth of an alligator snapping turtle, offered my blood to leeches, or put my toe before the toe biter... and who would've thought that this barrage of bites would become such an entertaining and educational way to share animals with the world?

The Beast of Bites takes you back to the heart-racing and sometimes bloody moments we all enjoyed on the *Brave Wilderness* YouTube channel. The thing that's different is that this time I am taking you behind the scenes to share many of the elements that didn't appear on screen. From concept to creation, adventure to creature capture, and finally the science and psychology of putting myself through these oftentimes horrific scenarios.

Do you have any idea of how hard it is to place

a giant desert centipede on your arm and make it bite you? No, probably not, and I hope you never do! Remember...*never* repeat any of the ridiculous stunts I perform. My team and I do an incredible amount of research before filming these episodes, and we always seek out the advice of animal and medical experts before ever putting me in harm's way.

Each chapter is filled with edge-of-your-seat adventure and suspense, but we have also added in a ranking system known as the Savage Scale!

FEAR: The *anticipation* of what will happen (1–5)
IMPACT: The moment of biting impact, and my first impression (1–5)
DAMAGE: The resulting trauma directly after the bite has taken place (1–5)
AFTERMATH: The long-lasting and even permanent effects from the encounter (1–5)

You will see this laid out at the beginning of each chapter to help us break down the four basic aspects (Fear, Impact, Damage, and Aftermath) of every painful experience. Each category is worth 1–5 points—1 being the lowest, and 5 being the highest—and when all categories are added together, we have our Savage Rank, which can be anywhere from 4–20. No two bites are the same, and hopefully the Savage Scale will add a little extra fun for those that love to measure the wrath I have endured throughout my adventures.

Everyone always asks, "Coyote, will you ever be bitten by a (*insert any animal species here*)?" As of now, my goal is to no longer take any extreme intentional bites or stings. Believe it or not, I actually do my best to *not* be bitten! After all, if you're a wildlife presenter and are constantly getting bitten by the animals...you're probably not that good at your job! However, accidental bites do happen and since this book was written, I have been bitten in the face by a nine-foot carpet

python, chomped by a frilled dragon, sliced open by a piranha, and taste tested by a yacare caiman!

Now, kick back and enjoy *The Beast of Bites*....This is going to be one wild adventure!

Pain is nothing more than a test of one's might, and once it has been overcome, the adventurer hails tougher than ever before.

—Coyote Peterson

CHAPTER 1

CHOMPED BY A SWAMP DRAGON!

ALLIGATOR SNAPPING TURTLE

SAVAGE SCALE

FEAR	✴	✴	✴	✴	✴
IMPACT	✴	✴	✴	✴	✴
DAMAGE	✴	✴	✴	✴	✴
AFTERMATH	✴	✴	✴	✴	✴

TOTAL: 14/20

If you're reading this book, it is very likely that you have seen an episode of *Dragon Tails* on the Brave Wilderness YouTube channel. *Dragon Tails* is a series that highlights my favorite animal in the world: the snapping turtle. Now, some of you may be saying, *Coyote, what's so great about a turtle?* The real question is, what isn't?

Snapping turtles are the apex predators of whatever body of water they have chosen to call home, be that a swamp, pond, river, stream,

or lake. They have perfect camouflage, hunt with stealth and precision, eat anything that moves, and have several impressive defensive characteristics. Growing up in rural northeastern Ohio, I was absolutely captivated by them.

There are two widely recognized species of snapping turtle: the common snapping turtle and the alligator snapping turtle. The common snapper, which I proudly nicknamed the mud dragon, can be found pretty much anywhere in the United States east of the Mississippi River, whereas the alligator snapping turtle is only found in the southeastern United States.

Catching my first mud dragon at the age of eight was like winning my first trophy, and it sparked my thirst for adventure and broadened my perspective about wildlife. Since that day, I have had the same enthusiasm and admiration for these swamp

creatures and am always on the lookout for the next big mud dragon.

Now, this chapter is about the *alligator* snapping turtle...so why am I talking about the *common* one? Because! They're both super cool!

I'm kidding! Although that is true, it's because this is a bites book, and before I ever *intentionally* got bitten by a common snapping turtle—there were a few accidental ones—I went arm-to-beak with the bigger, spikier, heavier alligator snapping turtle.

Now, you may be asking, *Coyote, why on earth would you do that?!* Well, let's start at the beginning.

SHREVEPORT, LOUISIANA

In the summer of 2015, the Brave Wilderness team and I traveled to Shreveport, Louisiana in hopes of finding and catching one of the largest freshwater turtle species in the world: the alligator snapping turtle. Aside from my general fascination with these reptiles, I was particularly interested in the rumors surrounding them.

I'd read countless stories of fishermen pulling up turtles who weighed over two hundred pounds, and I was greatly intrigued by Loch Ness monster–like folklore from Indiana called the Beast of Busco. This turtle of legend was supposedly the size of a small car, but despite elaborate efforts, it was never caught and officially recorded. One of the oldest turtle tales on record dates back to 1937 and describes a 405-pound beast caught in Kansas. However, without any photos or official documentation of the catch, this behemoth remains only the subject of lore.

When it came to Louisiana, it seemed like almost everyone had a gator-snapper story to tell, and if only a handful of these stories were true, it meant that big turtles could still be found lurking in these southern swamps. Well...there was only one way to find out. To try my luck at landing a giant, I had to travel to the giant's lair.

Located in the southeastern United States, Louisiana features the perfect habitat for these ancient-looking reptiles. Nicknamed the Bayou State, this area contains around 45 percent of the wetlands found in the Southeast, so of course it would be an ideal place to find massive snapping turtles.

The state of Louisiana could be described as one giant wetland, or—to use the language of Louisiana—a bayou. The great Mississippi River flows all the way from northern Minnesota to the

Gulf of Mexico, slowing once it reaches, you guessed it, Louisiana. The tide from the Gulf pushes against the flow of the water from the Mississippi, causing it to flood over its banks into the surrounding land. All that water and silt settle in the woodlands, creating a five-million-acre delta.

Our plan was to work with a local wildlife enthusiast and alligator-snapping-turtle expert, Adam Remedies. Locally known as the Turtle Man of Louisiana, Adam has been safe-trapping these snappers for several years and, like me, has a profound admiration and respect for these amazing reptiles. When we reached his location, he greeted us with five awesome specimens happily resting in a large containment pool full of cool water.

After scouting the location and getting hands-on with a few of Adam's resident turtles, we filmed an episode comparing the most significant features of both the common snapping turtle and alligator snapping turtle. The most obvious difference between them is the sheer size and weight of the alligator snapping turtle's body, head, and, most important, jaws. The wide spread of its mouth, dagger-like points on its beak, and crushing jawbones make up a formidable combination.

I suppose I could say that my curiosity got the best of me, because after filming that segment, I couldn't stop asking myself, *Just how strong* is *that viselike bite?*

Even though we had a handful of great animals to film, I wanted to explore the murky streams and rivers, find the heaviest alligator snapping turtle possible, and catch it by hand. As I previously mentioned, Adam typically uses a technique called

HOOP NET

safe trapping, which utilizes hoop nets to immobilize turtles without causing them harm. *My* tried-and-true method is to kayak out into a body of water, look for signs of turtles, and then jump right on top of my target to catch it before it dives for the mud or darts away. I was determined to utilize my own experience to catch a giant alligator snapping turtle in the estuaries of Louisiana, but I quickly learned why Adam uses hoop nets.

Unlike common snapping turtles, alligator snapping turtles prefer the deep water of rivers or lakes to the shallow water of ponds and swamps. All the locations where Adam caught massive sixty-, eighty-, and even hundred-pound turtles were deep pockets of murky water along the banks of rivers. Instead of actively searching for food, alligator snapping turtles are ambush predators, meaning that they hunker down on the riverbed, mouth agape, waiting for a meal to swim by. Inside their huge mouths, they have a fleshy, wormlike pink appendage called a lure, and by waggling it, they entice fish

FUN FACT!

The method alligator snappers use to draw in prey is called lingual luring. *Lingual*, meaning "tongue," because of the lure in their mouths!

to swim right up to their jaws. Once one gets close enough...*WHAM!* They snap their beak shut and—*GULP!* —it's mealtime!

Like all turtles and tortoises, alligator snapping turtles have beaks instead of teeth, so instead of chewing up their food, they have to swallow it whole. What if they catch something too big for one gulp? Well, at the tip of their beaks they have two pincerlike

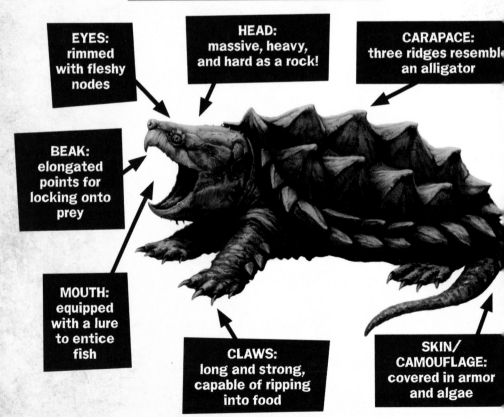

ALLIGATOR SNAPPING TURTLE
MACROCHELYS TEMMINCKII

EYES: rimmed with fleshy nodes

HEAD: massive, heavy, and hard as a rock!

CARAPACE: three ridges resembl an alligator

BEAK: elongated points for locking onto prey

MOUTH: equipped with a lure to entice fish

CLAWS: long and strong, capable of ripping into food

SKIN/ CAMOUFLAGE: covered in armor and algae

points that they use to lock onto their prey, giving them time to work their mouths like shears to break apart their prey. Once it's in pieces, they gulp it down bite by bite. Sounds gross, right? But it's these special features that

have allowed the alligator snapping turtle to not only survive but thrive for millions of years!

That's right! Fossil records from the Cretaceous period show that the alligator snapping turtle has been on this planet, nearly unchanged, since the time of the dinosaurs! When you look at their heavily armored shells, bearlike claws, massive size, and strength, it's easy to see why these amazing beasts have no rivals among their territories. Since they spend most of their time at the bottom of the water, algae grow thick on their carapace and heads, allowing them to blend in perfectly with their environment. Unfortunately, none of these characteristics help adult alligator snapping turtles survive against their only predator: humans.

FUN FACT!

The alligator snapping turtle has several defensive behaviors. They will first try to flee, then show their huge jaws, let out a scary hiss, snap at anything within range of their mouths, and secrete a stinky musk!

Alligator snapping turtles are an unfortunate victim of overharvesting and poaching. Ever heard of turtle soup? Before they were identified as a federally threatened species, alligator snapping turtles were a main source of meat for communities all over the southeastern United States. What's worse is that their environment has been drastically changed as well. The interwoven river systems have become polluted by heavy gas and oil extraction, and man-made structures such as canals, dams, levees, and corridors have structurally changed the natural flow of their habitat. These turtles are incredibly long-lived and can reach ages of over one hundred years, yet those ancient individuals are extremely rare due to illegal harvesting and environmental encroachment.

I paddled, waded, and drifted along the river, searching for hours until the sun began to set, but in the end, I had absolutely nothing to show for it. According to Adam, alligator snapping turtles become much more active at night, so my best chance at getting hands-on with a beast of the bayou would be at dusk. I wasn't going to give up.

As darkness blanketed the environment, I abandoned my kayak and shuffled waist-deep in the slow-moving water, looking for any sign of a

carapace. When my boot felt something hard and ridged beneath me, I reached below the surface, felt the unique ridges of the shell, and grabbed ahold of a heavy turtle trying to make his escape.

"*GOTCHA!*" I exclaimed. Yet again, my proven method of catching snapping turtles had won me my victory! I marveled at the sixty-pound turtle as I brought him up to the surface. His mouth was characteristically wide open, revealing the impressive spread of jaws. Again, the thought crept back into my mind: *I wonder what a bite from this beast could do to my arm....*

The next day, I decided to rely on my two most-trusted cohorts to push me in the right direction. Mark—the fearless director of the Brave Wilderness channel—and Mario—our experienced wildlife biologist and trusted voice of reason—were always on hand to lend their insights on my craziest ideas.

"What would you guys think about me testing out the strength of a bite from an alligator snapping turtle?" I asked them as we packed our gear for another full day of filming.

WHAT'S IN THE NAME?

Unlike their common cousins, alligator snapping turtles have three ridges on their shells, called keels, resembling the backs of alligators!

"Like, with your arm?" Mario laughed. "I don't know if that's such a good idea."

"It'll be fine!" joked Mark. "Let's do it!"

Clearly, they did not help my state of indecision. Someone had to break the tie, so I turned to the most dedicated and committed members of the audience for guidance: the Coyote Pack.

Later that day—May 2, 2015—I posted a picture of the sixty-pound alligator snapping turtle and posed this question: *Should I or should I NOT do a small featurette on what it's like to be bitten...yes, BITTEN... by an alligator snapping turtle?* I decided that the voice of the majority would determine if we filmed the episode or abandoned the idea... at least temporarily.

coyotepeterson

Since we would have to film this scene the very next day, we knew we had to do some serious preparation to keep me and our star snapper safe. Regardless of the Instagram response, *I* was

still curious about the power of jaws, and I racked my brain trying to come up with a way to demonstrate the force of that beast's bite.

As I walked the aisles of a local grocery store, inspiration struck. There was a huge selection of turkey legs in the meat section...and they were about as big around as my forearm. *Score!* I thought. *This would be perfect!* Mark and Mario were looking for something that could act as a shield for my arm, in the instance that the Coyote Pack begged for the bite.

When we met up in the checkout line, I had several turkey legs and a bamboo pole to hold them packed in my cart. I wouldn't want to get my fingers close to that beak, so for this presentation, I'd jam the turkey leg into the bamboo, keeping myself at a safe distance. Mark and Mario rolled up with some paint stirrers, bamboo stakes, Ace bandages, and athletic

tape to construct some sort of brace for my arm, *if* I was going to take a bite.

When I woke up the next morning, I bolted straight out of bed to check my phone, anxiously anticipating my fate for the day. Eagerly, I scrolled through the comments, counting each response, and tallied them up at the end. *Oh boy*, I thought. *Looks like the Coyote Pack has spoken!* The majority was overwhelmingly in favor of the bite! Some of you were concerned for my safety (thank you), but due to our late-night grocery run, we had all the safety precautions covered.

I set my phone down and immediately notified Mark and Mario of the response, sealing our plans. There was no turning back. It was time to face the crushing jaws of the snapper!

––––––

Obviously, I wasn't going to get bitten by the biggest alligator snapping turtle we caught, but I still wanted it to be impressive. Luckily, Adam had a few on his property who were the perfect size for such an experiment.

We had all the accessories we would need; we had the turtle, and we had the approval of our audience. Suddenly, as we began setting the scene, I sensed a sneaking feeling of anxiety creep up my spine. *Wait, am I really going through with this?!*

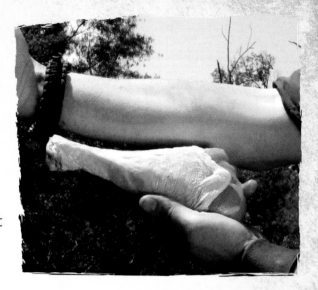

"You think this is crazy, right, Adam?" I asked, reaching for a turkey leg.

"Yeah, I wouldn't do it," he said, shaking his head.

Next to my arm, the turkey leg would be the best way to gauge the power of this reptile and could potentially be a fail-safe to pump the brakes on taking a bite if we sensed that it was too dangerous. It was just as thick as my forearm, with a sturdy bone running through the middle. I wedged the leg bone into the hollow end of the bamboo rod, fastening them together with an extra shoelace I had in my pack.

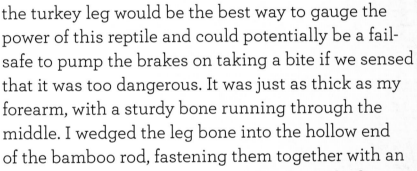

FUN FACT!

Alligator snapping turtles are omnivores, and in addition to fish, they also eat nuts, berries, aquatic plants, other turtles, and even small alligators!

Adam brought the fifty-pound alligator snapping turtle over and set him down on top of a cooler. His massive carapace covered the entire lid, and he slowly lifted his

23

head, jaws wide open in a defensive position.

"Are we ready?" I said. "This is an alligator snapping turtle biting down on a turkey leg."

I moved the meat into the bite zone, and in a split second...*CRUNCH*. His scissorlike beak clamped down onto the bone, with a very audible snap and crunch resounding from the trial turkey leg. *CRACK*. He let up pressure, then redoubled his grip, grinding the leg bone over...and over....

"Oh my gosh," I said. "Did you see how deep his beak went into that meat?!" *GURGLE*. My stomach turned over. Immediately, I knew there was no way my arm could sustain the pressure and damage that this reptile was clearly capable of inflicting. "I don't know about this, guys," I said. "Let's rethink this."

The alligator snapping turtle has a bite force of

Man, look at that bite! It sounds like a meat cleaver coming down.

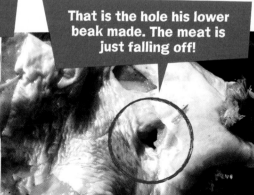

That is the hole his lower beak made. The meat is just falling off!

nearly one thousand pounds per square inch, so there was no way I was putting my arm into the viselike mouth of this creature unprotected. Luckily, we had already prepared a brace for my arm.

"You only grow one set of fingers," Adam said. "Just remember that." We wrapped an Ace bandage around my arm—to keep my skin from bulging under the pressure of the bite—reinforced in four corners by splints of bamboo. Then, to give it all a level of stability, keep the brace in place, and provide extra protection, we wrapped everything in multiple layers of athletic tape. With the freshly fashioned brace now secured to my arm, I felt a little better.

Kids, never try this at home!

"Kids, never try this at home," I warned, examining the strength of the cast we built.

Now it was time to reset our scene. We rinsed the turtle's mouth with bottled water, removing any leftover meat or bamboo debris. I got another look at the inside of his huge mouth, which was completely unscathed by the turkey leg. *CHOMP!* He clamped down on the bottle. Clearly, everything that got too close was fair game for a massive bite.

DID YOU KNOW?

Adult alligator snapping turtles have no natural predators, but baby alligator snapping turtles can be food for raccoons, herons, alligators, large fish, foxes, and other alligator snapping turtles!

This might be my craziest idea yet, I thought, replaying the scene and sounds of the turkey leg in my mind as I prepared to

take on the jaws of the alligator snapping turtle. Would it slice through my flesh with ease? Would it puncture my muscle? Could it even break my bones?

The human forearm has two bones: the radius and the ulna. The radius is much thicker than the ulna near the wrist and can withstand more force. If one of these bones were to break, it would probably be the ulna. With that in mind, I had to strategically place my arm in the reptile's mouth with the stronger bone taking the brunt of the impact from his jaws. I would be taking the bite on my right (and dominant) arm, which is the stronger of the two. If I wanted to minimize damage to me *and* the turtle, I'd have to hold out my right arm well away from my body.

RADIUS

ULNA

The clock was ticking down. I had a GoPro strapped to my wrist to capture an up-close look at the action. The alligator snapping turtle was in place, his mouth freshly

rinsed out, and his menacing jaws gaping wide open. Adam stood behind him, ready to wrangle the reptile if things went south. I wiped the sweat from my forehead and took a deep breath. *There's no turning back, Coyote. You can do this.*

My heart was racing, and I could feel a giant lump of nervousness stuck in my throat. Anxiety ran up my neck and buzzed through my brain, as though every ounce of my body were begging me not to go through with it. I stubbornly delivered my signature intro, my arm held out in front of me.

"I'm Coyote Peterson," I said to the camera, "and I'm about to enter the Strike Zone with the alligator snapping turtle. Adam, you ready?"

He nodded.

"Mark? You ready?"

Thumbs-up.

I reached over with my left hand and patted the turtle's head, prompting him to open his mouth as wide as he could. "One, two, THREE!" *WHAM!* I thrust my arm into his mouth,

WHAM!

CRUNCH

and then *CRACK!* Immediately, he bit down and snapped one of the bamboo braces, but he didn't stop there. He let up and—*CRUNCH!*—bit down again.

"AH! GAH!" I yelled. The pressure was immense and was all I could think about as the turtle continued to wrench down on the brace.

"OW! GEEZ!" I felt the distinctly sharp points on his beak pierce the athletic tape, but I couldn't take out my arm. If I tried to remove it too quickly, his jaws would lock into place, and I would end up dragging my skin through the knifelike points of his beak.

CRACK! "Ooh! I can hear him cracking the bamboo!" I grunted, and just as I was about to call it quits, he heaved his massive head to the side and clenched

CRACK

down again, this time right in the soft muscle on the edge of my arm. *Just what I was hoping to avoid!*

Before my mind could even process the thought, my body jerked back my arm, away from the jaws of the alligator snapping turtle. "He's through, he's through, he's through into my arm!" I gasped. "Aw, geez, he went right past the bamboo and into my arm."

You know that feeling you get right after you hurt yourself doing something your mom would definitely tell you not to do? You know how your head gets hot, your eyes start to water, and you get a giant lump in your throat that screams regret? Well, I do.

"I can definitely feel it," I said, squeezing the torn-up brace on my arm. It's hard to describe the feeling

My arm is throbbing!

of ten consecutive chomps by a creature with a bite force that rivals a lion's. I could feel throbbing pain down to my bone. Hot, dull pressure swelled beneath the brace. My thoughts were racing as I tried to predict what my arm looked like without

being able to see under the cast. Maybe I had deep gashes, or punctures and dark-purple bruises. Or maybe all that pressure ended up breaking the bone! I was in so much pain, that when Mark asked if I was okay, I could barely put together a sentence.

The adrenaline was surging throughout my body, causing my stomach to do flip-flops and my vision to blur. When I was finally able to piece the words together, I began to look over the damage.

"Yeah, I think his beak definitely went down through this. You can see the hole right where he slipped in between the bamboo...," I said, my arm shaking, "...and went into my arm." I took a few deep breaths and ran my fingers over the brace.

"The pressure was unlike anything I've ever had on my arm before...and I could feel the weight of it really stressing the bamboo—about to its maximum." My eyes darted to the frayed athletic tape.

Keep it together, Coyote!

"It wasn't until he got over to the side and his beak pierced through that—" Just replaying that image in my mind sent a heavy wave of pain up my arm and into my stomach. *Keep it together,* I told myself. I don't know if it was the heat and humidity, the adrenaline, or the pain, but I felt as if I was going to be sick every time I recalled the moment when his beak sunk into my skin. As the seconds ticked by, the throbbing in my arm got worse and worse. It felt as if my flesh wanted to burst out of the brace, and I had reached my limit.

"Can we cut and get this thing off of me?" I said, removing the GoPro from my wrist. "I feel like it's cutting off my circulation, and it's making me feel sick."

I wanted to tear off the athletic tape, fling

the bamboo into the bushes, and peel
back the Ace wrap as fast as possible. In
no time, everyone dropped what they
were doing and came to help. Mark and
Adam unwrapped the brace while Mario
unzipped our first-aid kit. I couldn't have been
more thankful to have such an amazing team
that always has my back—supporting me through all
my wildest ideas.

As you can imagine, my arm was still in one piece,
but dotted with painful, deep punctures from the tip
of the turtle's beak. After we released the alligator
snapping turtle back to his watery home, I spent
the rest of the day with ice packs and bandages...
and a heavy respect for the creature who had left a

DRAGON DAMAGE!

permanent mark on my arm. Later that day, dark-red and purple bruises formed under my skin and swelled until you couldn't see the shape of my wrist. Though no bones were broken, and I didn't need stitches, I can't even begin to imagine what would have happened *without* the bamboo brace.

Before releasing our star, the alligator snapping turtle (who I appropriately named Big Chomper), I thanked him for being such a good sport. Because of the few hours he spent with us, Big Chomper taught over twenty-five million people about the strength and power of alligator snapping turtles, why they should be revered, and how important it is to admire these dinosaurs of the swamp from a safe distance.

The stories and legends that led me to Louisiana may have been tall tales, but they definitely illustrate the impact these beasts of the bayou leave with anyone who is fortunate enough to see them in the wild. The bite of the alligator snapping turtle secured its place in history as the first time Coyote Peterson was ever *intentionally* bitten by an animal for the Brave Wilderness channel, but as you all know, it certainly would *not* be the last.

CHAPTER 2

FRESHWATER BLOOD FEAST!

LEECHES

SAVAGE SCALE

FEAR	✸	✸	✸	✸	✸
IMPACT	✸	✸	✸	✸	✸
DAMAGE	✸	✸	✸	✸	✸
AFTERMATH	✸	✸	✸	✸	✸

TOTAL: 13/20

One of my favorite things to do as a kid was exploring the swamps and creeks near my home, searching for big bullfrogs, slimy salamanders, and, my favorite reptiles of all, turtles. When I spotted a cool aquatic creature, I would leap into the murky water without hesitation. While I was waist-deep in swampy muck, however, a creepy thought nagged at the back of my mind.

There's something that lurks in the shadows of the swamp, something you've seen on other animals but

DID YOU KNOW?

The word *leech* comes from the old English word *laece*, meaning "physician."

have never been able to find alone, and something that magically finds YOU....This mysterious and squirmy creature who haunted me was the humble **LEECH**. I rarely thought about them *before* setting out on an adventure, but once my clothes were soaked, a sneaking paranoia would take hold.

What I didn't realize as a kid is that there are no freshwater species who prey upon warm-blooded creatures like mammals (or small children, like me) in my region of northern Ohio. The handful of leech species where I grew up primarily sought cold-blooded creatures like turtles or frogs, or other aquatic creatures like fish and snails. As a young explorer, however, the nightmare of being devoured by leeches seemed just as real as getting swarmed by pesky mosquitos.

As an adult who still loves exploring swamps and ponds in Ohio, I have had several encounters with leeches in the wild. When I started making content for the Brave Wilderness YouTube channel, every time I would catch a snapping turtle, I would gently pull off any leeches in sight before releasing it back into the water. Leeches are parasites who feed off the turtles'

blood, and even though they do not harm their hosts, I feel like I'm doing a Good Turtle Samaritan thing by removing those leeches whenever I see them.

After two seasons of *Dragon Tails*, I started to notice a common question asked by the Coyote Pack: *Coyote, how many times have you jumped in to catch a snapping turtle and come out covered in leeches?* Actually, in all my years of exploring freshwater ponds, lakes, and rivers in the United States, I have never found a single leech **FEASTING ON MY BLOOD**. After seeing these questions time and time again, I started to wonder... *why haven't I ever been bitten by leeches?* To investigate,

FUN FACT!

All blood-sucking leeches have special saliva.

I started to look into these creepy-crawlies a little further.

After a quick search on the internet, I discovered horrifying accounts of kids and adults going for a freshwater dip and emerging covered in these squishy-squirmies. In one story, a few hikers who briefly waded through a slow-moving, shallow river recalled finding them buried in their socks and shoes! In another encounter, after just fifteen minutes of swimming, the author became a host to forty-four leeches! *YIKES!*

Aside from these firsthand tales of **PARASITIC ENCOUNTERS**, I also discovered why I'd never played host to a family of leeches. There are around 680 known species of leeches in the world, and out of those, only about 80 species live in North America. Of all leech species, only 75 percent are **hematophagous**, meaning that they feed on blood. Fewer than 25 percent of bloodsuckers, however, will actually seek out a human host.

Leeches can be found on

WHOA!

The largest leech in the world is the giant Amazon leech (*Haementeria ghilianii*), which can grow up to eighteen inches and live up to twenty years!

HOW DO YOU SAY THAT?

Hematophagous:
"he-mah-toe-FAY-gus"

every continent except Antarctica and come in many varieties, each type having a very specialized diet. Some are scavengers, consuming decaying plant and animal material in ponds and swamps; some seek out small invertebrates like insect larvae and snails; and some have a particular taste for the blood of fish, turtles, frogs, and other aquatic inhabitants.

HOW DO YOU SAY THAT?

Proboscis:
"pro-BAH-skiss"

It all depends on their environment and their mouths. Out of nearly seven hundred known species, three-quarters are jawless leeches and are either scavengers, parasitic, or predatory. Parasitic jawless leeches use a **proboscis** to access their hosts, which include the variety of aquatic creatures I just mentioned. Predatory leeches don't have jaws or a proboscis, but instead have an enlarged mouth that they use to consume their prey whole! This includes insect larvae, small worms, and mollusks.

CONTRACTED PEAR-SHAPED LEECH

Leeches' bodies are also very different from one species to another. Some are sausage-shaped, while others are pear-shaped with tiny heads at the front and round suckers at their back. With amazingly flexible bodies, they can change their shape to suit their behavior. When leeches are planted on an object or animal, their bodies are contracted and broad, whereas if they are swimming, they extend their bodies to become long, flat, and streamlined.

So now you know that not all leeches suck blood, and not all blood-sucking leeches seek the blood of humans! *But what about the ones who do?!* I'm sure that's what most of you are *really* interested in. Most of the leeches who fall into this category belong to the subclass Hirudinea, and many of them are equipped with **JAWS AND TEETH**. These leeches live all over the world and thrive on land as well as in aquatic habitats, but true land leeches feed *only* on the blood of mammals and birds and are only found in moist climates close to the equator.

One of the most well-known and well-studied leeches of all is the infamous *Hirudo medicinalis*, or **EUROPEAN MEDICINAL LEECH**, found originally in the southwestern regions of Europe and the Mediterranean. Yes, you read that right: **MEDICINAL LEECH**. Leeches have been used to treat various conditions and diseases for thousands of years. The science behind their

application has changed dramatically over time, but they have consistently been counted on for **LEECHING**, a practice thought to relieve illness from the days of the ancient Roman Empire until the Middle Ages.

Can you imagine going to the doctor for a headache and getting a prescription for two leeches?! Although they aren't really used to treat headaches anymore (but they were!), they are still used in medical procedures today.

So, what does all of this have to do with Coyote Peterson getting eaten alive by leeches? Well, in early May 2016, I had a particularly eventful day at one of my favorite Columbus and Franklin County Metro Parks: Ashton Pond at Blacklick Woods, Ohio. I was hoping to see a huge snapping turtle who I had encountered the previous year, but I ended up landing a behemoth who I had never caught before. What I was not expecting that day was that I also caught a few huge leeches hitching a ride on the snapper express. Through the tussle of hoisting the turtle onto my trusty kayak, he scratched my hand with his long claws, and soon I felt the presence of a visitor I had never expected...a leech.

While I was holding on to the carapace, a big goober of a leech slowly crept onto my hand, so I had to show it off to the Coyote Pack. I noticed that even though it seemed attracted by my minor snapper injury, it wasn't biting me. *Hmm...I wonder what it would take to actually get eaten alive by leeches*, I thought. *Better ask my audience!*

On the spot, I made a fateful post on Instagram:

After just a few days, the results were in. *YES! Coyote, we want to see what would happen if you got eaten alive by leeches!* I mean, who wouldn't?

Those of you who were concerned for my safety, fear not. If I was going to actually deliver on this episode, I was going to set it up like a proper experiment. My goal was to show the Coyote Pack that most species of leech will not seek out human hosts, but what

coyotepeterson

Liked by **thousands of others**

coyotepeterson Dragon damage... leech buffet... would anyone like to see us do an episode on leeches and their ability to syphon blood from their victims? Lets put it do a vote and see where it lands me 😊 🐉

to expect and how to remove it properly if you happen to get bitten by one. That meant I had to do lots of research, gather information, and, most important, find out how to get ahold of some leeches. Much to my surprise, it really wasn't that hard.

Since leeches are available for medical purposes as well as for scientific research, I contacted a laboratory about the most common leech used for medical purposes: the European medicinal leech. In hospitals, they are used to treat patients who have undergone microsurgery and vascular surgery to initiate good blood flow in damaged tissue.

The European medicinal leech, *Hirudo medicinalis*, produces a very efficient and strong anticoagulant in its saliva called hirudin, which prevents blood from clotting.

Have you ever scraped your knee or elbow from a fall? Well, think back to the moment when you first inspected your injury. At the injury site, your raw pink skin may have been bleeding a little. After several minutes (and probably a Band-Aid), the bleeding stopped because blood clots had formed around the injured area, blocking blood from flowing freely. Whenever the body senses an injury, it sends special cells to the site. These cells not only stop bleeding, but also prevent invasion from bacteria and promote healing. This special component produced by leeches—hirudin—prevents those clots from forming.

Now, you may be thinking, *But, Coyote, don't you want to stop bleeding?* Not always! Microsurgery is a very special type of surgery that is performed to

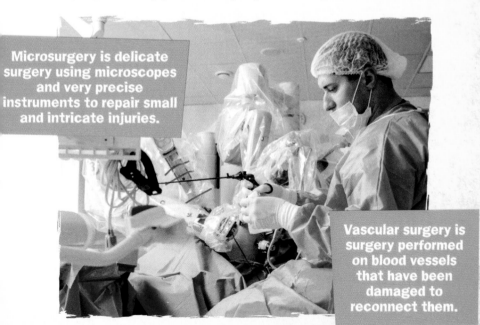

Microsurgery is delicate surgery using microscopes and very precise instruments to repair small and intricate injuries.

Vascular surgery is surgery performed on blood vessels that have been damaged to reconnect them.

reattach fingers, repair life-threatening wounds, or fix important organs and tissue after scary things like tumors are removed. While the body heals, it's vital that these injured areas get good blood circulation, and if the blood starts clotting, there can be major problems.

COLUMBUS, OHIO

After talking to lab experts, I got my hands on two leech species for our episode, ensuring that they didn't carry any blood from previous hosts, bacteria from their environment, or parasites that might find Coyote Peterson to be a suitable new home. Safety first!

After two months of research and a very special internet order, I was ready to fulfill my promise to the Coyote Pack. On a bright, humid July morning in 2016, the Brave Wilderness team and I set out to make one of the most **EERIE AND BIZARRE** episodes yet.

EW EW EW!

EUROPEAN MEDICINAL LEECHES

COMMON FRESHWATER LEECHES

The two different leech species I had on hand were the previously mentioned European medicinal leech and a common freshwater leech, each in separate jugs. The freshwater leeches are native to North America, and their favorite foods include the blood of fish, amphibians, and turtles. The medicinal leeches, which are native to Europe, don't prefer fish at all. Their favorite food is...**HUMAN BLOOD**. To illustrate these differences, I was going to submerge my arm into a container of water with these creepy creatures for fifteen full minutes, giving them plenty of time to attach themselves.

First, Mark, Mario, and I would be testing the tastes of the common freshwater leech. Well, let me be clear: Mark and Mario would be filming; *I* was the only one with my arm in the water. I had a couple GoPros ready to capture footage underwater, but I felt pretty confident that there wouldn't be much exciting action. I looked at their long, flat brown bodies, and shuddered. No matter how unlikely it was, thinking about them sticking their **NEEDLELIKE PROBOSCIS** under my skin gave me the creeps.

"All right," I said, rolling up my sleeves. "It's time to empty the freshwater leeches into the container." I poured the entire contents of their plastic jug into the tub before me and peered down at them as they explored their unfamiliar environment. *They're actually kind of elegant.* They swam like rippling ribbons, cutting through the water with ease.

"Moment of truth," I said to the camera. "I'm about to stick my arm into the container with freshwater leeches." Kneeling just behind the container, I laid my hand and arm into the tepid water and silently lowered it. The leeches seemed to take notice and immediately landed on the plastic bottom close to my arm, sealed to the basin with their suction cups.

Wait, suction cups? Well, actually they are called suckers. All leeches have two suckers—one in the front and one at the back—and these mechanisms are what help them navigate their environment and latch onto surfaces. They can attach and detach each end at will and can even crawl along their environments like inchworms. Some leeches have prominent suckers on both their heads and tails (like the hungry European leeches), while most leeches, like the ones who were swiftly swimming around my arm, have one big tail sucker and tiny head suckers.

As I looked into the watery basin, one found its footing in the tub and was slowing creeping toward me.

"What do we have here! One of them might attach!" I said, surprised. A few were suctioned to the bottom of the container, just a hair from my arm, waving their heads through the water and scanning my warm skin. One by one they curiously inspected this unknown fleshy thing in their environment, but each leech turned away. Eventually, they all sought

No, thanks, Coyote.

Got any frogs?

out small areas of shade and settled down out of the sun. Clearly, they wanted nothing to do with me or my blood. The experiment—however uneventful—was a success. We proved that given plenty of time and opportunity, common freshwater leeches will not latch onto human skin and drink blood.

On to the next phase of the experiment.

We plucked the freshwater leeches out of the basin, plopped them back into their original home, and set them in the shade. Next, I turned my attention

to the speckled leeches, currently clinging to the sides of their container. *Oh boy,* I thought. **IT'S TIME TO LET THE VAMPIRES OUT.**

I felt a sneaky nervous sensation prickling up my arms and began tinkering with the GoPros to buy myself some time. Mario watched me set and reset the same camera in the water three different times and stared at me with a smirk on his face and his arms crossed.

"Coyote, you're not *nervous*, are you?" he asked, trying to sound annoying.

"I don't see you volunteering to stick your arm into the water with leeches, Mario," I replied. But he was right. I picked up the leeches and unscrewed the lid, staring down at the wriggling, dark noodle-like creatures. The longer I looked, the more apprehensive my thoughts became. I screwed the lid back on.

"I am actually nervous at this point," I admitted. And for good reason! Based on my research, I was absolutely sure that every one of these twelve leeches was going to adhere to my arm and **CONSUME MY BLOOD**. Who wouldn't be nervous? "The leeches haven't eaten in a few days and trust me when I say... they are hungry."

I took a deep breath, wrangling my shaky thoughts and bringing my primary goal back into focus: I was doing this to educate the Coyote Pack, and to show them that leeches are relatively

They are hungry.

harmless and that they are nothing to be afraid of! I was determined not to let my nervousness get the best of me, so I knelt in the grass and took my place behind the leech display.

"You ready for me to put them in the container, Mark?" I said.

"Ready. Release the beasts!" he replied, his camera pointed directly at the tub in front of me. I unscrewed the lid and emptied the contents, watching all twelve leeches plop into the water. *Ugh!* My stomach couldn't help turning over as they spread out, squirming around the plastic in search of a meal.

"There's a lot of leeches in there," Mark noted as I looked up at him. The cringy expression on his face pretty much described how I felt: totally grossed out.

Before my mind could catch up with my body, I was standing. *Oh my gosh oh my gosh.* My mind was pleading with me not to subject myself to what would be one of the grossest things I've ever done.

Deep breaths, Coyote.

Everything was ready, everything was set, and all I had to do was submerge my arm and take the painless bites of these creatures. *Deep breath*. I rolled up my sleeve past my elbow, as high as it could go. *Deep breath*. I took my place once again. *Deep breath*.

"All right, so without further ado...," I said, taking a final gasp. "I'm Coyote Peterson, and I'm about to get eaten alive by leeches. One...two...here we go. Three." I slowly lowered my arm down, feeling the cool water slip over my skin.

The leeches immediately sensed that something new had entered their environment, and one of them made a beeline right for my arm. Although leeches have three to five pairs of eyes, they don't find food by sight. Instead, they are attracted to potential hosts by vibrations in the water and the smell of their chemical signatures. When I put my arm into their

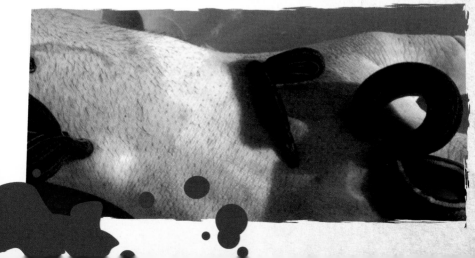

environment, disturbing the water, the hungry creatures homed in on my scent and followed it straight to me.

"Just like that!" I said, completely astonished. "Instantaneously, it's already secured to my arm." The leech reached out with its front sucker and grabbed on to me, then pulled its rear sucker in right behind it, making a fleshy brown loop. Not even five seconds later, three more found their way to me and were using their acute senses of touch and taste to latch onto the right spot and dig in to their dinner.

"Holy mackerel!" I couldn't believe how quickly they zeroed in on their meal. "Boom! Another on my hand." It was a feeding frenzy! At this point, I couldn't tell whether they had broken through my skin, because I wasn't feeling any pain. As soon as I focused on one, carefully watching to see what it

was doing, another would attach, and within sixty seconds all but one had adhered to my arm, wrist, and hand.

"Ack! *Sssst!*" I rasped, sucking air through my teeth. I could definitely feel something happening... though I wouldn't say it was painful. Just above my wrist, four of the leeches latched onto about two square inches of space. I don't know if it was because they were all so close together or if my brain was so acutely focused on feeling something, but I started to notice a gritty, scraping sensation like course sandpaper grinding down into my skin.

But wait...sandpaper? If they suck blood, don't they have teeth like a vampire?! Well, not exactly. This species, the European medicinal leech, does in fact have jaws and teeth, but they are unlike anything you can imagine. Leeches don't use their teeth to chew or tear like other animals. Instead, they have three ridged, bladelike jaws with one hundred little razor-sharp, pointed teeth on each. When the leech

opens its mouth, the jaws emerge like the petals of a blooming flower, looking like the letter *Y* when they are ready to sink into the host.

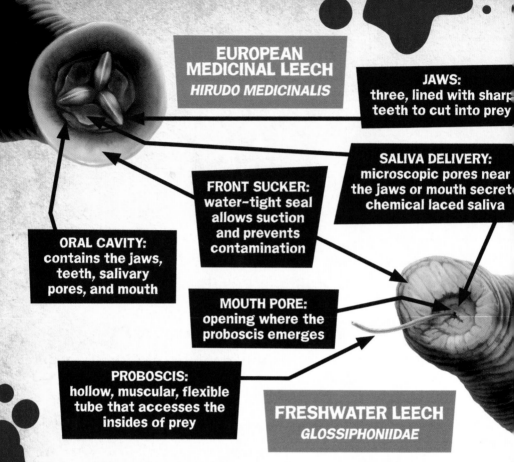

EUROPEAN MEDICINAL LEECH
HIRUDO MEDICINALIS

JAWS: three, lined with sharp teeth to cut into prey

SALIVA DELIVERY: microscopic pores near the jaws or mouth secrete chemical laced saliva

FRONT SUCKER: water-tight seal allows suction and prevents contamination

ORAL CAVITY: contains the jaws, teeth, salivary pores, and mouth

MOUTH PORE: opening where the proboscis emerges

PROBOSCIS: hollow, muscular, flexible tube that accesses the insides of prey

FRESHWATER LEECH
GLOSSIPHONIIDAE

Remember when I talked about jawless leeches? The common freshwater leech who I used in the first experiment is an example of the jawless parasitic leech and has what is called a mouth pore in the middle of a very small front sucker. In order to adhere to its host, it opens its mouth pore to reveal a needle-like proboscis, which it uses like a straw to suck the blood of its aquatic hosts. It, too, has special chemicals in its saliva, which it uses in the same way the medicinal leech does.

When one of these different leeches finds a

good spot to access the blood of its host, it creates a watertight seal using its front sucker, preventing water from diluting its dinner. Then the leech opens its mouth, revealing either its serrated jaws or its sipping straw, and, with surgical precision, presses it into the skin of its host, slicing through just enough to access its target: **BLOOD!**

"I can feel them cutting into my arm," I said, counting the bent-over wormlike creatures now firmly attached to me. I could see all twelve of them swelling up like water balloons, or should I say **BLOOD BALLOONS**. At this point, the leeches had only been on for a few minutes, and the more I thought about what they were doing, the more unsettled my stomach became. I wasn't in pain, and I wasn't scared of them, but as I watched them grow and contract, I started to feel a little queasy.

Ssst! I can feel those jaws!

"Holy cow, is this uncomfortable," I groaned, unable to take my eyes off them. *GURGLE.* I could feel my stomach lurching, and I was starting to get a little light-headed. "I think I need to turn the cameras off for a little bit." No questions asked, Mark and Mario down put their cameras.

Once I got over the initial shock of the leeches biting into my skin and my stomach settled, I was able to observe them in a different way. *They're actually pretty amazing creatures,* I thought. And they are!

If you really think about it, leeches are perfectly evolved predators. Without a skeletal structure or exoskeleton, they can squeeze through almost any opening, transform their bodies to suit their behavior, and can expand up to ten times their original size when consuming a meal!

WHOA!

European medicinal leeches can go up to eighteen months without feeding!

When they feed (which only happens about once a year), three important components of their saliva activate to make the processes as efficient as possible: (1) an **anesthetic**, a chemical that numbs the area; (2) a **vasodilator**, a special **enzyme** that causes blood vessels to get bigger; and (3) an **anticoagulant**, a strong enzyme that keeps blood flowing by preventing clots from forming.

Because of these three components, the leech

can go undetected and undisturbed until it has finished its meal. Then it simply drops from its host as painlessly as it attached and seeks a dark hiding place in the water to digest its meal. Pretty amazing if you ask me.

"Coyote, it's been over fifteen minutes," said Mario. "Are you going to let them keep going?"

"Oh, really?" Time flies when you're getting eaten alive by leeches! "No, let's roll cameras and get these things off of me," I insisted. Even though I knew they

weren't hurting me and they could only consume about a teaspoon to a tablespoon of blood each, I was still very much looking forward to ending this experiment. Once Mark and Mario resumed filming, I faced the cameras.

"It's been about twenty minutes," I said, "And look at how big these leeches have gotten. **THEY ARE COMPLETELY SWOLLEN WITH BLOOD AT THIS POINT.**

Dinner's over buddy!

"At this juncture, I think the leeches have had enough of a feast. It's time to get them off my hand and arm." I delicately raised my limb out of the tub. *Oh my gosh.* A few of the leeches looked like they were about ten times bigger than when we started and seemed to struggle to keep ahold of my skin. Finally, it was time to show the Coyote Pack the proper way to remove an unwanted parasite.

"There is a right way and a wrong way to remove a leech from your body," I explained. "You may think, *Let me yank it off.* Yanking it off is bad, because you can actually pull their teeth out into the wound. If those teeth get left in the wound, you can end up with an infection." *Although I can certainly understand the temptation,* I thought, scanning over the **PLUMP BLOOD SAUSAGES** swaying on my arm. There is really only one proper way to remove a leech, because attempting to scare it, pull it, or hurt it while it is still attached can have worse consequences than the bite itself.

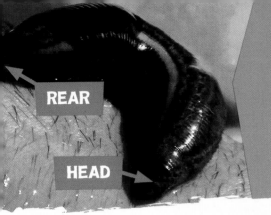

HOW TO TELL THE DIFFERENCE!

The head sucker of the leech is smaller than the rear sucker, and the body should be slightly narrower near the head.

REAR

HEAD

"The best way to remove a leech," I said, eager to demonstrate, "is to just use the edge of your finger." On the knuckle of my right hand sat the mouth of one of the fattest leeches I had on me. "What I want to do is softly slide the anterior sucker off of the wound." I started to gently push my thumb forward when Mark raised a very good question.

"How do you know which one is which?" he asked, just in time.

Just as I was starting to explain the difference, the leech's rear sucker detached as if on cue. I delicately supported its body between my fingers, and the mouth immediately let go. "Oh! That one popped right off!" and then *PLOP!* Another leech tumbled off my hand, splashing into the water below. "Oop! And that one popped off, too."

"There's also the

That's a full leech!

instance when the leech has eaten enough and it releases itself on its own." I reached into the water and picked it up. *Weird. It feels like a squishy, firm, wet noodle...like a giant piece of macaroni.* "Look at how full that leech is. It is done eating." I didn't know if I was more repulsed or impressed.

To make matters worse, as soon as the leeches released their grip, **BRIGHT-RED BLOOD** began seeping steadily from my hand. Coyote Pack, if you're squeamish, I advise you to skip ahead a few pages. This chapter is about to get **GORY**.

I still had to demonstrate a proper leech removal, so I focused my attention away from my bloody hand and up my arm. I carefully positioned my finger right at the base of the front sucker and carefully slid my fingernail across my skin, lifting up the sucker. The leech was reluctant to let go, but with a steady push, it finally released its grasp. After the front sucker is removed, all you have to do is pop off the rear sucker and you're home free!

One by one, I slid each of the remaining leeches off my skin using this same method, and one by one, they plopped back into the water, still curled up like fat horseshoes.

"There you have it!" I beamed, stopping before evicting the last one. "You guys ready?" I called to the cameras as I triumphantly slid my thumbnail under the front sucker. "Dinner's over, buddy." With one final push, the last leech let go. *PLOP!*

What a relief! My nightmare seemed to finally be over! I gazed down at my arm, now streaked bright red from the wounds left by my unwanted dinner guests.

"My blood looks really, really thin," I remarked, "almost watery. That's because of the amount of anticoagulant that went into my hand." The hirudin compound produced by the leeches can stay active in tissue for twelve to twenty-four hours in a laboratory setting. This, unfortunately, was not a laboratory

setting. I knew I'd be bleeding into the next day.

Despite my red leaks, I wasn't really feeling any pain. If anything, my arm felt numb and heavy as I held it up in front of me. My hand, which seemed to be bleeding the most, felt like a stiff deadweight on my wrist, and it was hard to move freely.

I took a deep breath through my nose and picked up on the metallic smell of the **BLOOD-TAINTED WATER**.

GROSS!

"Look at how red the water is," I said. Through the red haze in the water, you could still make out bright speckling on the backs of the leeches. While before the speckles on the leeches appeared pumpkin orange, they were now as **RED AS THE BLOOD ON MY ARM**. "It's like a shark attack!" Drip by drip, blood ran down my arm and rolled off my fingertips and into the water, each drop leaving a curling red ring in its wake.

My head was starting to feel a little fuzzy, and after a long morning, it was time to wrap up our experiment. We set out to show our audience that not all leeches will bite, and that the ones who do cause very little to no pain. We were also able to successfully demonstrate how to properly remove a leech and what to expect when you have been bitten. The last step after we were done filming was to show the Coyote Pack how to properly treat a leech bite, and then it was time for a little rest!

Be Brave...
Stay Wild!

"I'm Coyote Peterson," I said, giving my final send-off. "Be Brave...Stay Wild—we'll see ya on the next adventure!" I stood up, walked off camera, and then—whoopsie!—quickly sat back down. *I think I got up too fast*, I thought, feeling a little woozy. Mark immediately got up and came to check on me. The little bit of blood that I lost from the leeches was tiny compared to my total blood volume, so I wasn't worried about my safety. But anytime you see and smell your own blood, it can make you feel a little out of sorts.

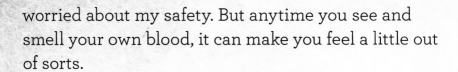

"You ready to start cleaning up?" Mark asked, keeping a close eye on me. Boy, was I! We quickly gathered up all the leeches, put them back in their container, and put the rest of the bloody mess in biohazard bags. The set was cleaned up, so I took my place in front of the camera, blood still oozing slowly down my arm.

"Today I'm going to show you how to clean up a leech bite," I said cheerfully, "or twelve." Since none of us are medical professionals, Mark, Mario, and I wanted to give a brief demonstration of how to apply basic first aid to the bites.

"If you are bitten by something even as simple as a leech, seek medical attention if you feel you need it," I stated. In my backpack, I had all the essentials: Band-Aids, antibacterial wet wipes, hydrogen peroxide spray, and antibiotic ointment (Neosporin). I also had plenty of paper towels and water, which I would use to clean my arm first. The blood had started to dry, and in order for the Band-Aids to stick properly, they had to adhere to a clean surface. I poured water all over my arm and hand, thinking that it would wash right off, but it didn't. As I rubbed, I ended up smearing it all over the place! *This is harder than I thought!* I probably should have brought soap.

Once I finished rinsing off, I grabbed a handful of paper towels and dried the area. Immediately, the small wounds started bleeding again.

"Look at that, you can see where the exact bite zones are!" I said, watching blood seep out of the bite sites. "Isn't that crazy? Gosh, it just won't stop...."

On to the next step. I grabbed the wet wipes and began quickly wiping the affected areas. The wet wipes would clear away any bacteria from the wounds and help prevent infection. *"Ahhh!* That stings!" I continued my treatment with a little hydrogen peroxide, another quick wipe-up with paper towels,

and finally I seemed to be making some progress.

"The bleeding seems to have slowed down," I continued. Before bringing out the bandages, I ripped up a clean paper towel and stuck the pieces on each bite. After a few minutes, it was time for the final step!

"The next thing I'm going to use is Neosporin and, because this is a *Dragon Tails* episode, Ninja Turtles Band-Aids." I squeezed the jellylike ointment out onto each bite and rubbed it in. Then I picked out my favorite ninja bandage (the red-wearing Raphael of course!), and carefully applied it over the ointment. *Hmm...this isn't working as well as I'd hoped.* Despite all the cleaning, the paper towels, and the ointment, the bandages weren't sticking! *Sorry, Raphael.*

Time for plan B: gauze and medical tape. I unpacked the gauze, which is a roll of breathable cotton, and stuck it to my hand with tape. Then I carefully wound the bandage around my hand and up to my elbow, just tight enough to keep pressure on each incision. No muss, no fuss! Things don't always work out as well as you would like them to, and when you're in the field, you need to improvise!

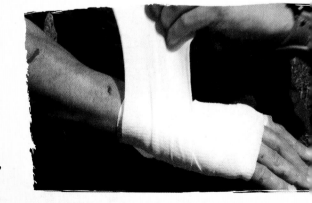

Finally, we were done! The whole process of setting up the leech experiment, getting up close

WHOA!

It took around forty-eight hours for all the leech bites to stop bleeding completely!

to the aftermath, cleaning up the set, treating my wounds, and packing up took the Brave Wilderness team and I several hours, and I was ready for a little downtime.

The leeches we used to film this episode couldn't be released into the wild, as they came from a laboratory. I will never harm any animal in order to make an episode, so I donated them to a local medical facility, where they aided in furthering research about their potent saliva.

After twenty-four hours, some bites were still bleeding, while others looked like the Mercedes Benz logo!

When the Brave Wilderness team and I set out to show our audience the effects of leech bites, we were well prepared for the bloody aftermath. Through careful and thorough research, I was fully aware of what I was getting myself into. I always make sure my friends, my crew, and I are safe, and would never put myself at greater risk than I can handle.

That said, I think I missed the part of my research that said that leech bites itch like crazy a few hours later. When I performed a routine change to my bandages, I had to add a little anti-itch cream to the bites because *man, oh man!* They were driving me totally crazy.

I hope that by reading this chapter, you have learned a little bit more about leeches. Most of

them are completely
harmless, even in the
rare instances that
you sustain a bite. It
takes a little patience,
a few bandages, and a
lot of understanding to
properly handle a leech

encounter, but it's not something you ever need to fear.

CHAPTER 3

ATTACKED BY AN ATTACK DOG!

BELGIAN MALINOIS

SAVAGE SCALE

FEAR	✸ ✸ ✸ ✸ ✸
IMPACT	✸ ✸ ✸ ✸ ✸
DAMAGE	✸ ✸ ✸ ✸ ✸
AFTERMATH	✸ ✸ ✸ ✸ ✸

TOTAL: 12/20

For many people living around the world, dogs are man's best friends. They live in our homes, protect our families, and show unconditional love and understanding. They enjoy long naps with their favorite humans, trips to the park with their favorite ball, and a nice big bowl of their favorite food. Some of you, however, may view canines not with admiration, but with fear. I'm talking about **cynophobia**, or the fear of dogs. Although not as common as **arachnophobia**

(fear of spiders) or **ophidiophobia** (fear of snakes), cynophobia can be much more debilitating. According to the National Pet Owners Survey, 48 percent of households in the United States have at least one dog, resulting in a national dog population of about seventy-seven million and counting!

HOW DO YOU SAY THAT?

Cynophobia:
"sin-na-FO-bi-a"

Arachnophobia:
"ah-RACK-na-FO-bia"

Ophidiophobia:
"oh-FID-ee-oh-FO-bia"

Imagine the animal who you are most afraid of, then imagine being confronted by it in every park, on every neighborhood sidewalk, and in half of all homes. It would be hard to leave the house! Not everyone who is wary of dogs will flee at first sight, but for some, even a happy, puffy ten-pound poodle will incite as much fear as a rampaging bear. All it takes is one bad encounter.

It may surprise you to learn this, Coyote Pack, but I know firsthand what that's like. I don't fear every dog who crosses my path, but if I ever see one without a collar and without a human companion, I keep my distance. I've never personally been bitten, but when I was a kid, a friend of mine suffered a significant attack from a stray dog that put him in the hospital and left him with many stitches. I happened to be there to witness the event, and the fear I had in that moment sticks with me to this day.

Of course, stray or feral dogs are not the same as family companions, and not all strays are dangerous. When I was a kid growing up at home, my mom raised golden retrievers, and I never felt uneasy or on guard around them. A big and fluffy, goofy, poufy golden retriever who has spent a lifetime in a loving home is a lot different than a stray who might never have known human care and affection. Often, stray dogs are just scared and wouldn't normally approach an unfamiliar person.

Now I am the proud owner of a happy, silly brown dog named Charlie Bear, who loves nothing more than a good day with her family, chasing after

CHARLIE BEAR

balls in the backyard and receiving nighttime snuggles. But even though I have had plenty of great experiences with dogs, just one bad one will always keep me on my guard. In order to be safe, Coyote Pack, never approach a wandering dog, even if it's wearing a collar.

Humans have had a long history with dogs creating close ties over thousands of years. A now-extinct primitive species of wolf is thought to be the first animal domesticated by humans, which scientists believe occurred up to fifteen thousand years ago! As hunter-gatherers, humans developed cooperative relationships with canines. Over time, these relationships grew closer and more intertwined, making dogs essential to our lives. Because of their incredible senses, drive and focus, and their friendly dispositions, dogs work in a broad range of industries, just like people.

Dogs aid farmers by herding livestock, fending off predators, and guiding lost animals back home.

DID YOU KNOW?
Dogs have forty-two permanent teeth in their mouths! The tiny ones in the front are incisors, the long ones are canines, and the back teeth are molars!

As companions, they assist with everyday tasks for those without sight, hearing, or the use of their limbs. As medical assist dogs, they can detect seizures before they happen and abnormal heart rhythms, and some even specialize in detecting bacteria, viruses, and cancer. In law enforcement, dogs' keen sense of smell allows them to sense everything from narcotics to electronics to gems or precious metals. They can be trained to track people in any number of difficult situations, including search-and-rescue operations in the aftermath of natural disasters. As technology advances and training methods improve, dogs are becoming more and more adaptive to our changing world.

The Brave Wilderness team and I wanted to know firsthand what it was like to train with a

DID YOU KNOW?

The domestication of dogs occurred in different places all over the world, in places like Egypt, Japan, Northern Europe, China, and East Africa.

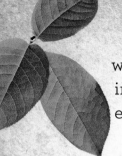

working dog, and luckily, we had just met some incredible people who were enthusiastic and experienced K9 specialists.

When I was contacted by the professionals at Makor K9 of West Virginia, I was very intrigued by what they had in mind: *Hey, Coyote, would you ever consider wearing an attack suit and letting*  *one of our dogs take you down?* Wait, what? *Attack suit?!* That's right. The specialists at Makor train dogs for law enforcement, protection, and detection. After thirty-five years of hard work, Makor K9 has earned a worldwide reputation as one of the top K9 specialist training organizations in the world.

The amazing Makor canines work alongside humans and provide canine-specific services. For example, humans don't have noses keen enough to detect bombs or illegal substances, but dogs do! Humans can't follow a scent trail in the wilderness to find a lost or injured person, but dogs can! But how do they learn those skills? Can *any* dog be a police dog?

These are exactly the same questions I had the first time I spoke with Jay Kerr, a co-owner of Makor K9.

"While there are many excellent dog breeds out there, the most common ones used in law enforcement are the German shepherd, Dutch shepherd, and Belgian Malinois," he explained. *Belgian Mal-in-laws? What is that?!* I wondered. (Don't worry—you'll learn more about this incredible animal as you keep reading.) Jay continued to reveal that Makor is very selective about the dogs they choose to train, and they spend countless hours testing potential candidates before selecting just a few.

"A good candidate has to be focused, fearless, and—most important— friendly," he continued. "We look for dogs with high endurance, high drive, and an enthusiasm to learn. The worst thing you can have in a working

dog is crittering." *Another word I don't understand. Crittering, like chasing critters?*

"Crittering is a behavior that most dogs have, where they'll get distracted by the smell or movement of a small animal and ignore their handler" *Oh...well, my dog is definitely out. Sorry, Charlie!*

The more I spoke with Jay on the phone, the more excited I was to see one of these amazing animals in person, so we set a date to meet.

WEST VIRGINIA

On a beautiful, sunny summer morning in West Virginia, Mark, Mario, and I drove down country roads to meet our new friend Jay and his best friend, Maya. Maya is Jay's canine companion and is one of Makor's representatives and demonstrators. She has been trained in odor detection, tracking, and apprehension, a skill I was bound to learn more about.

As we pulled up to a little-known park Makor often uses for canine demonstrations, our tires skidding on the gravel parking lot, I wondered what I was in for. *It looks like there are a lot of people here,* I thought. *I hope it all goes according to plan.*

There were groups of excited spectators scattered around a pavilion that sat in the middle of a long field, and they were all there to see a spectacular takedown. Jay greeted us as we unloaded our vehicle, shaking each of our hands with enthusiasm. He introduced us to the other trainer we'd be working with, Nathan Jackson, who rushed over from a table covered in thick, padded jackets. We walked around and met some of the spectators, law enforcement officers, and K9-unit specialists, and then it dawned on me. *Where's the dog?*

"I'll get Maya out before we get started," said Jay, almost reading my mind. "Let's talk about what we will be doing first." He walked me over to the pavilion and pointed out across a hundred-yard field. I would be positioned about fifty yards out, start running, and then Maya would be given the command to chase.

WHOA!

The canine with the strongest bite force is the Kangal shepherd dog, reaching just under 750 pounds per square inch of pressure!

"You'll be wearing protective gear, but when she makes contact, she will do everything she can to bring you down," Jay said casually. "Once you tell us to stop, we will give her the command to release."

I had never worked with a professionally trained dog before, but I had seen firsthand what kind of damage an aggressive dog could do if it was in full-on attack mode. Confronted with the thought of

experiencing that myself, I started to get a little nervous. I paused, trying to think of the best way to tell him what I was worried about.

"She's definitely going to let go, right?" I asked.

"Absolutely," Jay said firmly. "The exercise we'll be demonstrating today is like Maya's favorite game. Canines learn best when they're in a fun environment, so all our training exercises are designed around play. She may look angry and aggressive, but that's just a part of her training. As soon as she hears the command to stop, she will." Jay explained that Maya had been rehearsing this exercise every few days for the last three years. Her training grounds were always different, and she'd worked with countless individuals without incident. "Trust me, you're in good hands."

Before I met Maya, Jay told me a little bit more about her. Maya is a Belgian Malinois, one of the breeds favored by law enforcement organizations across the world. The Malinois resembles a German shepherd but smaller. They weigh about forty-five to fifty-five pounds, have light-brown mid-length fur, pointed ears, and dark markings around their eyes, ears, and muzzle. Their appearance can vary greatly depending on the region where they are born. Some have dark fur from toe to shoulder, some have dark chests, and some are almost completely black.

GERMAN SHEPHERD

BELGIAN MALINOIS

The Belgian Malinois was originally bred for herding livestock, but their high energy, endurance, and incredible focus have made them ideal candidates for law enforcement. All the dogs at Makor are born in various European countries and are carefully raised and trained basic obedience from birth. Specialized training begins when the dogs are twelve to eighteen months old, and they don't start working until they have mastered every skill in the training process.

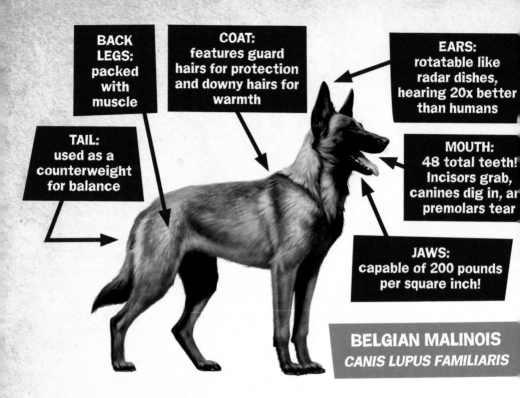

BACK LEGS: packed with muscle

COAT: features guard hairs for protection and downy hairs for warmth

EARS: rotatable like radar dishes, hearing 20x better than humans

TAIL: used as a counterweight for balance

MOUTH: 48 total teeth! Incisors grab, canines dig in, ar premolars tear

JAWS: capable of 200 pounds per square inch!

BELGIAN MALINOIS
CANIS LUPUS FAMILIARIS

"Coyote, are you ready to get started?" Mark said, "We're all set up."

Ready or not, I can't back out now, I thought. I wasn't sure if I would ever really be ready to get taken down by an attack dog, but I was confident in the skills and expertise of Jay and the professionals gathered around me. *What could go wrong?*

I took my place next to Jay, and Mark gave us the signal that it was time for action.

"Today we are on location in West Virginia with Jay from Makor K9," I said to the camera. "And we're going to do something a little bit different today, aren't we?"

"Yup," Jay answered. This certainly wasn't the first bite episode the Brave Wilderness team had made, but normally we worked with *wild* animals. Today, we would be working with… what was this breed called again? "The Belgian Malinois."

"Maya, who is the dog we will be working with today, is actually really friendly as long as I don't have on the specialized suit—which is used to train her to do what?"

"Maya is trained in apprehension," Jay explained. This means she is trained to stop criminals in their tracks. These dogs work closely alongside law enforcement officers to locate and safely subdue people who have committed harmful crimes. "She worked law enforcement for four years, and now she works as a demonstration canine for our company."

"So today I'm going to be part of her exercise," I said. "And I will be at the receiving

end of today's demonstration to show exactly what this dog is capable of."

"You're going to be the victim," Jay said, smiling.

Victim?! I thought. *Isn't this supposed to be a game?!*

As Jay assured me before, I would be totally safe during the course of this exercise. That's partially because of the protective equipment I would be wearing. While preparing for the episode, Jay and I selected which specialized garment to use, as each piece of equipment offered different levels of protection. The full suit would cover my whole body and was thick with padding like a Michelin Man costume, while a jacket would cover just my torso and arms.

FULL SUIT

JACKET

All pieces of equipment they had were constructed by hand for precisely this type of training by Schweikert "hundesport" K9 out of Germany. Along with lots of padding and sturdy wool, they were built primarily out of a woven,

puncture-preventing
material called Kevlar.

Kevlar is a well-known
material often used in
protective armor such as
ballistic vests, combat
helmets, and firefighting

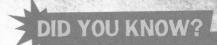

suits. Made of superstrong plastic, Kevlar is heat-
resistant, highly flexible, and versatile. When used
in protective equipment, millions of plastic threads
are tightly woven together in layers, making an
impenetrable barrier that can withstand anything
from blades to bullets to bites!

My goal was to run as far as possible before being
taken down, so the full suit would limit my mobility.
The jacket seemed like a good first option, and there
were two to choose from. *Shouldn't I pick the thickest
one?* I thought, pinching the
sleeves to test their padding. Jay
told me to choose whichever item
I was most comfortable with.

WOW!

Unlike other plastics,
Kevlar doesn't melt.
It decomposes at
around 850 degrees
Fahrenheit.

"It's up to you. You're the one
taking on the teeth," he said. "But
if you want to know what that jaw
pressure is really like, I'd go with
the thinner one. No matter which one you choose, the
dog will not be able to break skin on you." *Well, that's
reassuring*, I thought.

Beside the jackets lay a more streamlined option: tubelike padded sleeves. The sleeves are worn by themselves and would leave all the other parts of my body *not* covered by Kevlar exposed to potential damage. If I wanted the full experience, the sleeve would be the way to go. *I think we'll see how I do with the jacket first.*

"Bring on the jacket!" I instructed, gesturing to the hefty garment. I pulled it over my shoulders and beat my chest, imitating King Kong.

"That is legit!" I said, admiring my new attire.

I gripped the edge of my sleeve with my fingers, like a kid in an oversize coat. "Maya's not going to go for my fingers or my face, is she?"

This is legit!

"Absolutely not," Jay insisted.

"You're certain?" I said skeptically.

"Well...," Jay mused. "You have about one to two

percent chance she might go for the leg." I couldn't tell if he was joking or not.

TRRSCHT! I unfastened the Velcro and shrugged off the jacket, turning my attention to the slate-gray sleeve. It covered my arm from armpit to knuckles, had extra padding, and four cinching straps spaced evenly down the material. It was about seven pounds of pure protection, and even though it covered less, I felt it would offer more protection from the pressure of Maya's bite force.

PADDED SLEEVE

"Could she pull my arm out of its socket?" I asked.

"Hopefully not!" Jay joked.

"To be clear," Mark said, "tackling Coyote is actually fun for her, right?"

"It is absolutely fun. It's what she lives for," Jay replied. Maya is Jay's best four-legged friend, and I could tell he was excited to watch her play her favorite game. Since Maya is no longer a part of the law enforcement, she knows to never hurt a human for real. For her, these training exercises are a fun part of her daily routine. It's like playing ball with your dog at home...except I was going to be the ball that day.

Now it was time to meet Maya. Jacketless and sleeveless, I made my way across the field where the exercise would start. Nathan, one of the head trainers at Makor, walked out of sight to retrieve Maya from her traveling crate.

"They're getting Maya out of her crate right now... and I'm starting to get a little nervous," I said to the cameras. From a distance, all I could see next to Nathan was Maya's two upright pointed ears, swiveling like radar dishes as she trotted next to her handler. She was about two feet tall at the shoulder and weighed just over fifty-five pounds. As they got closer, I noticed that she stayed right by Nathan's side, constantly looking up at him for direction.

Once Maya got to the pavilion and I could see her more clearly, I realized: *She's as cute as a button!* With her tail wagging side to side and her tongue flopped over her chin, she didn't look scary at all. I felt a beaming sense of confidence soar through me,

and the previously unnerving scenario started to play out differently in my mind. *I'm pretty fast*, I told myself. *And pretty strong, too. At less than a third of my weight...she might not even be able to take me down!*

"*HOPP!*" yelled Jay from the pavilion. On cue, Maya effortlessly leaped onto a picnic table. "*PLATZ!*" he commanded, and Maya lay down. Because she was born in Germany, all Maya's training commands are given in German. She kept her eyes on Jay, and even when Mario got close with his camera, she never broke her focus.

"*Bleib,*" Jay said, and he walked away. Maya stayed exactly where she was and didn't move a muscle, even when he came back carrying her favorite toy: the protective gear. Nathan brought the jacket over to me, and I slipped my hands

COMMAND TRANSLATIONS

Hopp (hupp) means "jump."

Platz (plaatz) means "down."

Bleib (bliib) means "stay."

into the sleeves and shrugged it over my shoulders. From behind me, I could hear her breathing getting louder.

You know the frantic excitement of a dog when you bring out their toy? That innocent yearning in their eyes as they track every movement of your hand? That was what Maya was doing except, as I mentioned before, I was her ball.

"Kennel," Jay commanded in English. Without hesitation, Maya stepped off the table and slunk into her traveling crate, still breathing loudly with anticipation.

Whoa, buddy...she's really fired up! The confidence I was feeling before felt like it was slipping away, as I continued to hear the strained sounds of her excitement. I fastened the front of my jacket, pulled a GoPro vest over my head, and inched it down the oversize coat. *Here we go,* I said to myself as I clipped in the camera.

"All right, Jay, we ready?" I hollered. He gave a thumbs-up. "Let Maya out of her kennel."

"*Hier,*" Jay said, and she popped straight out. Jay held her collar and led her down the aisle between the picnic tables. With every step, she kicked off the concrete, ready to sprint straight for me. *PANT PANT PANT!*

"Hi, Maya!" I said meekly. *Oh boy.*

"*SITZ!*" Jay bellowed. Maya sat, panting and drooling, her eyes fixed on my every move. I held my forearm straight out in front of me, my right hand tightly gripping the end of the sleeve.

Right here, Maya!

"This arm, Maya, right here! This is the one that you want." I took ten steps back. *Here we go.* "I'm Coyote Peterson," I yelled nervously, "and I'm about to enter the Maul Zone with a canine." I took a deep breath, swallowed the lump in my throat, and tensed my legs, ready to take off.

"You ready?" I called. Mark, Mario, and Jay all nodded. "One, two...three!" I pushed off the ground and dashed away from them, barely hearing the strained whines from Maya as the wind rushed over my ears. My feet hammered into the soft grass, and I concentrated with all my might to keep my right arm out to the side as I fled.

For about four fleeting seconds, all I could hear was the accelerating *thump, thump, thump* of my pulse drumming in my ears, until faintly I caught Jay's voice giving another German command. *"Fass!"*

Instantly, I heard the unmistakable *da-dump, da-dump, da-dump* of Maya's paws hitting the ground, and the frantic *hah, hah, hah* of her breathing right before she leaped. For what felt like an eternity, an eerie silence blanketed the air as I looked over my right shoulder. She was

COMMAND TRANSLATIONS

Fass (fas) means "seek."

mid-spring on her back legs with her front paws forward, her mouth open, and her dark eyes fixated on her point of attack.

SLAM! Her front paws pounded into my back as her jaws locked onto my arm and stopped me in my tracks. In one smooth motion, she tilted her head and gained purchase farther down my sleeve, pulling me to my knees with all her weight. Maya took me down within one second.

"*ARRGH!*" I hollered instinctively. I could feel the points of her front teeth digging into my arm, and the rapid release and grab of her jaws as she changed her position. My feet were under my butt, slipping on the smooth grass, and I strained with every muscle in my body to resist her.

"*ACK! AHHH!*" I yelled through gritted teeth, trying to get my feet out from under me. Maya kept pulling me back, throwing me off balance, and

just when I thought I had enough purchase to stand, she swung her body to the right, twisting me around and forcing my knees back to the ground. She was crouched low, resisting every attempt I gave to free myself. *Holy cow! She's super powerful!*

"RRRRAGH!" I grunted as I fell forward. I felt myself getting dizzy and realized that Maya had spun me around in circles. As our duel continued, I wasn't focused on the sharp pain on my skin or the pressure that sank deep into my arm. My instincts kept my mind focused on my contender, and my eyes fixated on her every move. After another spin, I caught sight of Mark and Mario, frozen in place nearly fifty yards away.

"You comin' out here?!" I squawked. *BAM!* She jerked her head left and right, bringing my face inches from the ground. I used my free arm to push myself up, and saw Mark, Mario, and Jay hastily

shuffling across the field toward us.

"*AH! AH!* It hurts!" was all I could muster, and the pain in my arm grew. Throughout our entire battle,

Maya's jaws rapidly gnawed the sleeve, never relenting pressure. "*UUURRRGH!*" She took me for the ride of my life, and after just sixty seconds, I was so disoriented, I felt as if I were on the scrambler ride at the fair. I could feel a strained ache shooting through my shoulder from the constant left-to-right jerking of her head, and a crackling dull agony in my elbow as she continued to twist my arm back.

"Man!" I sputtered through deep breaths. "She is a lot stronger than you would think!" Now my left hip was on the ground, and instead of pulling away from her, I was actively trying to follow her motions just to ease the pain from her constant tugging. *Maybe if I heave my body upward, I can get back to my feet.* I gave it a feeble attempt, but I didn't have a chance. She spun me around 360 degrees in mid-lunge and took me down again. "*Arrrgh!*" I was nearly on all fours, until my free arm gave way.

"I could see," I breathed, "how this would easily"— GASP!—"easily take down a criminal! *ARRGH!*" One

more time, Coyote. Get back on your feet! RAAAGH!
Even my thoughts cried out as I pushed myself up.
With one last burst of strength, I engaged every
muscle in my legs, managed to stumble forward, and
fell straight back down to the ground. Finally, I was
ready to give up.

"Tap out!" called Mark as Maya wrestled me onto
my back. I peered over the tops of my knees at Jay,
desperately trying to make eye contact. He caught
my breathless request and
leaped into action.

"*AUS!*" he bellowed. "*AUS!*"
Miraculously, Maya let up
pressure on my arm and

**COMMAND
TRANSLATIONS**

Aus (ows) means "drop it."

backed away. She triumphantly trotted over to Jay,
looking very proud of herself. I knew the Kevlar
protected me from punctures, but my arm was
throbbing, so I sat up and looked over the jacket to
assess the damage.

"I could feel her teeth hitting the bones in my
elbow," I said, exhausted. "That hurt the worst." I was
breathing hard, as though I had just sprinted a mile,
and lay back down.

I picked myself up off the ground and yanked open
the jacket. After sliding my arms out, I immediately
noticed the damage. A dull throbbing sensation ran
from my fingers all the way up to my shoulder, and I
could feel distinct pressure points where the canines

gripped me especially hard.

"I definitely feel my arm swelling up," I said, breathing through my teeth. "You can see all these puncture marks." My skin was streaked with rough red drag lines, and in some places, I could see purple blood blisters taking shape.

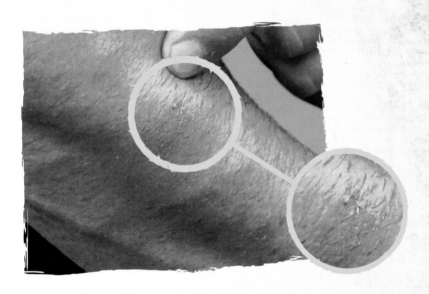

"I'm going to the sleeve," I said breathlessly, holding out my left arm. "Let's beat up both arms today." Jay placed the open sleeve under my left arm and fastened it closed with the Velcro cinch straps. Unlike the loose-fitting jacket, the sleeve was fastened down tight, meaning that there was less loose material for the Malinois's teeth to dig into.

"I may feel slightly more impact." I said as Jay called Maya over to her starting line. Mark and I

walked out fifty yards into the field, and I faced my foe once again.

"Let's do this," I said to Mark. Then I called out to Maya: "Maya! Right here! This arm right here—" Maya bent her head low, flatted her ears, and crossed fifty yards within a second. This time I faced her head-on, and when she made contact, she knocked me back several feet.

Immediately, she started dancing around me, knocking me off balance and twisting me around. Despite the extra padding, I could feel every jagged tooth as she ratcheted down on the sleeve. With every shake of Maya's head, every twist and turn, the force of her jaw seemed to get tighter.

"*AAH!*" I grunted, face-to-face with my attacker. Instead of looking vicious, Maya's bright eyes

gleamed with excitement, like a puppy with its toy, and her tail joyfully waved back and forth. The only sounds of growling were coming from me as I struggled against the incredible strength and agility of this amazing animal.

"I can feel—*arrgh!*" I grunted. "All the pressure of her teeth—*uuurgh*— going into my arm!" Round one lasted about ninety seconds, but after just thirty seconds in round two, I tapped out. "Okay! Get her off!"

Nathan rushed in and held her by the back of her collar as Jay called the command *"Aus,"* indicating that it was time to let go. She clearly wanted to keep the game going but released her jaws as she was hoisted back by her handlers, revealing the big, broad smile on her face.

I felt like I'd had the workout of a lifetime and gasped to catch my breath. I could tell from that exercise that what made Maya so effective at takedowns was not merely her body weight and strength, but her agility and ability to maneuver around her target, preventing them from getting the upper hand.

"That was as intense as it gets," I said. My teeth

were clenched, my brow was furrowed, and my mouth tight. "Much scarier to have the dog on your arm with no other protective body cover." I looked at the depressions in the material, noticing how close her teeth got to my exposed hands. Even though this was just a training exercise,  it pushed me to my limits not just physically but mentally, as I faced my long-standing fear of being attacked by an attack dog.

"That was absolutely an experience that I am never going to forget!" I pronounced. "I'm Coyote Peterson. Be Brave...Stay Wild—we'll see ya on the next location!"

My experience with a professionally trained canine far surpassed my expectations. Maya was so intelligent and focused that it was like working with a human. Every command was followed without hesitation, and even in the intensity of her training, Maya maintained an excited, playful demeanor.

Dogs like Maya are unique. They may seem robotic and cold to bystanders who see them at work, but every trained working dog knows the difference between work and play. And just like humans, they take their roles very seriously. As Jay would tell you, however, behind the scenes, these canines are just as friendly and happy as a family pet. To these brave animals, their jobs are their joy, and they enrich the lives of anyone lucky enough to be their partners.

It took a lot of courage for me to face my fears, and although I walked away with some swelling, bruises, and sore muscles, it was an incredibly positive experience. After breaking down our gear, I approached Maya without any equipment, and she happily greeted me with a smile.

"Okay!" Jay said to her. His last command told her that it was time to relax, that her work was done for the day, and that it was okay to just be a dog. For the rest of the afternoon, she enjoyed affectionate pets, fun games of fetch, and a few cuddles with none other than me, *her human chew toy.*

CHAPTER 4

ASSAULTED BY AN ALLIGATOR!

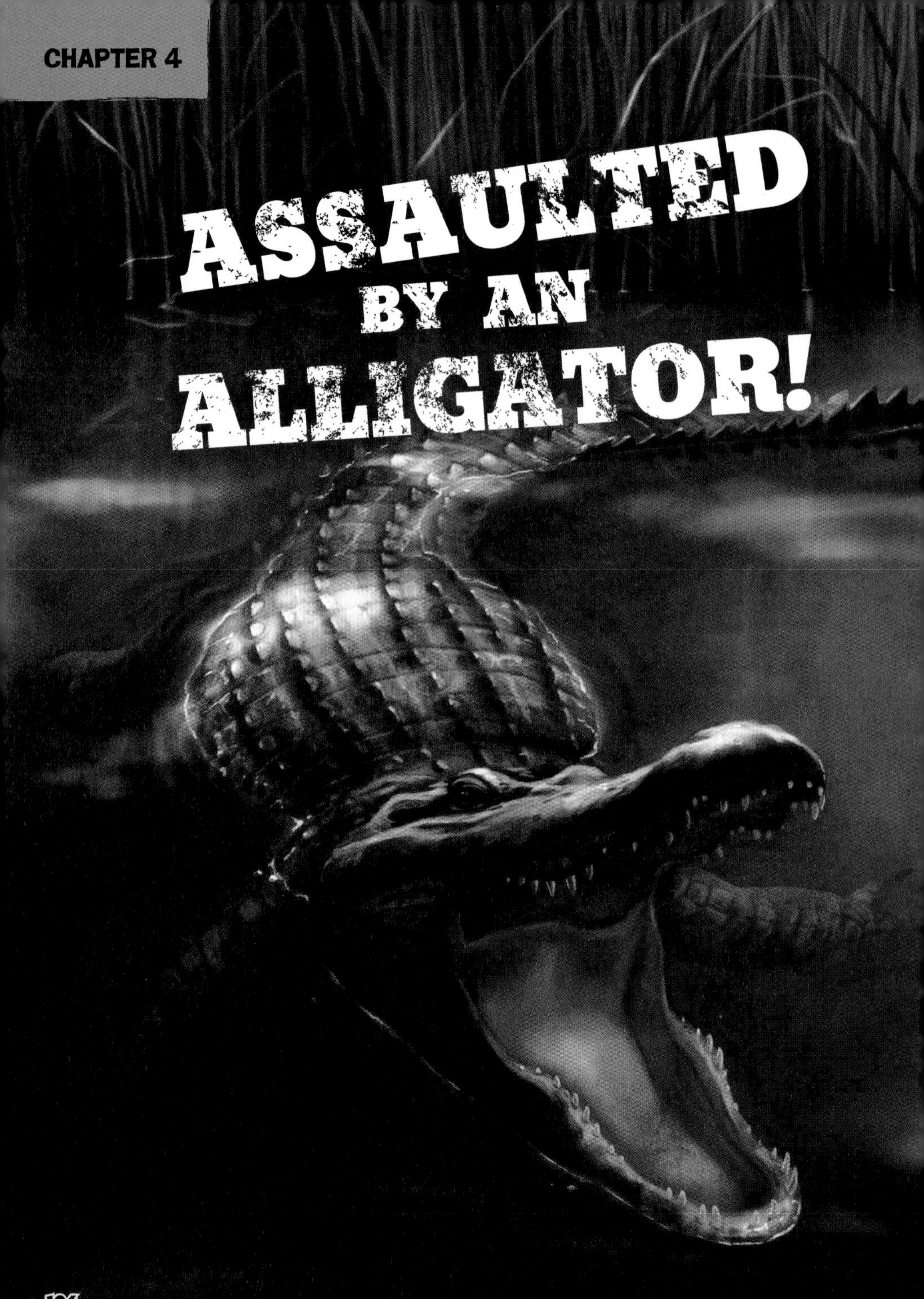

ALLIGATOR

SAVAGE SCALE

FEAR	✸	✸	✸	✸	✸
IMPACT	✸	✸	✸	✸	✸
DAMAGE	✸	✸	✸	✸	✸
AFTERMATH	✸	✸	✸	✸	✸

TOTAL: 16/20

When I was a kid, I loved going to pet stores. Every time my mom would take me, I would rush over to the reptiles and amphibians' section of enclosures to see what new and exciting things they had to offer. I would often press my hands up to the glass, searching for geckos hiding in their fake plants, or frogs sleeping in the shadows of their shelters. My favorite creatures to see, however, were the adorable baby alligators.

Oh boy, I wanted one so bad. I could distinctly imagine how much fun it would be watching it chomp down on hot dogs or putting it in the bathtub to scare my little sister. I'd tried explaining this to my mom, but no matter how much

I begged and pleaded, she would never let me get one. *Parents are no fun,* I'd thought at the time. Looking back on those moments, I can't thank her enough for standing her ground.

As an adult and a wildlife educator, I now know that alligators are arguably the worst reptiles you could possibly have as a pet. No matter how docile a pet alligator may seem, its instinctive nature still makes it incredibly unpredictable. Not only are they potentially dangerous pets, but they require an incredible amount of food and space. In just two years, an alligator can grow to over three feet in length!

Looks cute, right?

But an even larger concern is that when a pet alligator outgrows its enclosure, it can't be released outside. Not only is it unsafe for the alligator, it's even more unsafe for humans it may come into contact with! Unfortunately, that hasn't stopped many inexperienced alligator owners from releasing them in inappropriate places.

HOMESTEAD, FLORIDA

Mario, who was born and raised in Florida, worked with American alligators while earning his degree as a wildlife biologist. Through field and volunteer work, he helped relocate wild alligators who found themselves too close to human civilization by transporting them to wild habitats far from populated areas. Unfortunately, he encountered many gators who had grown accustomed to humans and couldn't be released.

"Even though it's illegal to own them without the proper permits, tons of people had them as pets," Mario explained, "and oftentimes, they would just release them out into local wetlands when they got too big."

That may not seem like a problem in

Florida, because they belong there, but it can be quite dangerous. Normally, when a wild alligator is approached by humans, it'll turn tail and skedaddle. However, alligators raised by human hands in captivity link humans with feeding time, no longer fearing them like their wild counterparts do, and they are likely to act aggressively for food. Their bottomless appetites trigger an instinctive feeding response, which incites them to take quick action to grab their meal no matter what or *who* it might be.

How can we film an episode about American alligators that encourages people not to get them as pets? we wondered. Then Mario had an idea.

"We should do a bite episode." *A bite episode?!* I thought. *Easy for you to say, Mario.*

"Think about it, Coyote!" He continued: "A juvenile gator would be the perfect size. We could film it at the Outpost!"

Mario's hope was that, by showing

a two-year-old juvenile on our YouTube channel, we would teach anyone considering a baby alligator for a pet that they don't stay small for very long. Alligators of any size are capable of doing damage, so it would be important to work with professional handlers we could trust. If we were going to film and carry out an alligator bite demonstration, the Everglades Outpost would be the best place to do it.

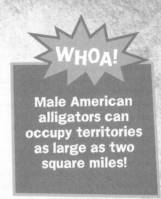

WHOA!

Male American alligators can occupy territories as large as two square miles!

As a volunteer, wildlife specialist, and wildlife educator, Mario had worked at the Outpost for about ten years before joining the crew at Brave Wilderness. We've been lucky enough to work with

the professionals there on several of our episodes and decided it was worth investigating.

The Everglades Outpost, or just Outpost as we call it, is a nonprofit wildlife sanctuary located in Homestead, Florida. The Outpost is an essential organization for the preservation of all Florida native species. The sanctuary houses everything from snapping turtles and snakes to Florida panthers and foxes, but they specialize in caring for Florida's most well-known reptiles: American alligators.

Along with the efforts of the Florida Fish and Wildlife Conservation Commission, the caring volunteers at the Outpost work to rehabilitate wild alligators and—if possible—release them back into the wild. As is often the case, however, they take in confiscated captive alligators, exotic pets, and non-native animals, too. The resources and professionals at the Outpost would be the perfect people to help us on our venture, but before we could make this happen, we needed permission from the Outpost's owner and operator, Bob Freer.

Right away, we called him to explain our idea. Bob fully supported the message we wanted to share with our audience but questioned our methods a bit. He probably thought our approach was absurd, but his trust and confidence in Mario won him over and he gave us the reply we were hoping for.

"All right, Mario, I guess that doesn't sound too bad. Come on down." Bob was on board! *How do I get myself into these things?!*

A few weeks later, in February 2016, Mark, Mario, and I packed our gear and set out for Homestead, Florida. We would need an entire day to film at the Outpost, so once we arrived, we plotted out the events of the following day, prepared our gear, and got a good night's rest. Early the next morning, we arrived on location, ready to set up.

We pulled up to the gate and heard the unmistakable voice of Bob Freer.

"I see you made it in one piece," he said. "Hopefully, you stay that way while you're here!"

Oh, Bob, always the joker. He led us through the sanctuary gate and

straight over to meet the gators.

We wanted to show our audience the size difference between alligators at each stage in their development, so we were looking for baby, juvenile, and adult candidates to film with. For the bite, I intended to use a juvenile who was about two years old, or around three feet, to show how much damage it could do after just a couple years in captivity.

ADULT — 10'

JUVENILE — 3'

HATCHLING — 12"

But what alligator episode would be complete without showing the impressive size and intimidating teeth of an adult?

Holy mackerel! I thought as we approached the first enclosure. *Those guys are huge!* The sun slipped over the palm trees in the sanctuary, blanketing the adult American alligator enclosure with warmth and bringing all the biggest males out to bask.

On the banks of a man-made alligator pond sat two giant gators, lazily soaking up the early morning sunlight. American alligators, like all reptiles,  are ectothermic, meaning that they absorb heat and energy from their environment. They were completely unfazed by us as we approached, refusing to give up their ideal spots.

"I see Godzilla is out," said Mario, pointing to one of the biggest males. Godzilla is a resident adult alligator at the Everglades Outpost and measures around ten feet in length. "He'd be a good one to work with if we need an adult."

Godzilla, seeming to agree, opened his wide jaws, showing off his impressive teeth.

"I won't be taking a bite from that guy." I laughed. "Let's see the juveniles."

Mario, knowing his way around the Outpost, led us over to a small pond where the young alligators were set aside. As we walked up, most darted into the water to hide, but a few of the bolder ones held their ground in the sun, eyeing us from the edge of the pond.

Juvenile alligators are one to three years old and can be anywhere from one foot to five feet in length. In this enclosure, there were six to choose from. The smallest was hiding underwater but looked to be about two feet long. The most outgoing was about three and a half feet in length and had already earned himself a nickname from the handlers at the Outpost.

"How about that one?" I asked, pointing him out.

"That's Junior," said Mario. "He's a little big, but Bob said he'd probably perform the best out of the bunch. You sure you don't want to use a smaller one?" Of all the young alligators we could choose from, Junior was the largest and wasn't afraid of humans. At just two years old, he was a perfect example of why alligators don't make good pets.

"I think it'll be okay," I said as I sidestepped along the bank of the enclosure, reached down, and grasped the young gator at the back of his neck. Junior tensed up and opened his jaws. *HISSS*, he warned as I carried him away from his enclosure. *THWACK!* He whipped his muscular tail back and forth, slapping me across the arms.

Oh jeez, he's definitely a lively one. Junior was a little bigger than what we'd planned for, but I still felt like he was the right representative for our audience to see how big American alligators get after just a few years of captive care. Still, being bitten by an alligator was a much more dangerous undertaking than being bitten by a snapping turtle, water snake, or lizard.

We had to plan our approach carefully to make sure I didn't experiene more damage than I could handle.

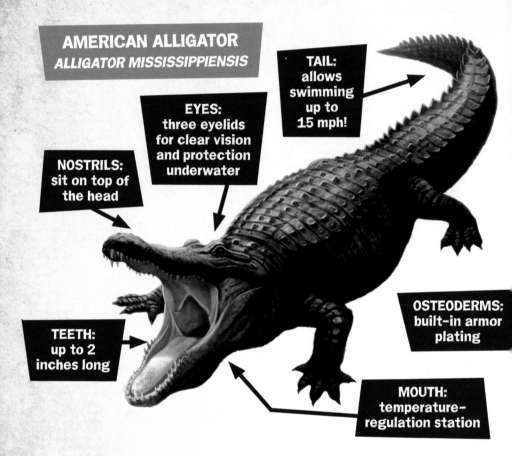

AMERICAN ALLIGATOR
ALLIGATOR MISSISSIPPIENSIS

TAIL: allows swimming up to 15 mph!

EYES: three eyelids for clear vision and protection underwater

NOSTRILS: sit on top of the head

TEETH: up to 2 inches long

OSTEODERMS: built-in armor plating

MOUTH: temperature-regulation station

The bite of an American alligator is potentially devastating for a few reasons. Their mouths are full of up to eighty sharp, jagged teeth with just enough space between them to accumulate bits of food. As the rotting pieces linger in their mouths, they accumulate a nasty concoction of bacteria that, while not harming the alligator, can cause a deadly infection in whatever they sink their teeth into.

Additionally, when a gator bites down, it doesn't let go. Once their jaws are locked on, they tense up their bodies, tighten their grip, and then explode instinctively into a barrel roll, taking their target by surprise, knocking them off balance, and ripping them to shreds. That barrel roll, or death roll as it is sometimes referred to, is exactly what I needed to avoid when I intentionally took a bite.

"We'll have someone hold him," said Mario. "He won't be able to do a barrel roll once he gets ahold of your arm." Mark looked skeptically over at us and gestured with his hands that he would definitely not be fulfilling the role of alligator handler.

As the sun continued rising toward its apex, we finished up our preparation and got in position to film a short introduction to the episode with Godzilla, the ten-foot alligator we saw earlier that morning. Godzilla was very used to working alongside humans for educational outreach and calmly sat on the bank of his enclosure as we set the scene.

"I'm just going to go right into it, ready?" I said, looking at Mark.

I crouched in front of Godzilla and stared into his gaping mouth, which was open wide and large enough to fit a whole watermelon inside. I teased that

I was about to thrust my arm between those jaws, stopping just a foot short of his snarly front teeth.

"I'm crazy, but I'm not that crazy," I joked to the camera. "What you're looking at there is over two hundred pounds of American alligator with one of the most powerful bite forces on the planet." Taking a bite from a full-grown gator like this would have irreparable consequences, which is why we were using a juvenile for the actual bite demonstration. If I took a bite from Godzilla...I'd probably lose my arm.

"I'm not willing to be bitten by an alligator of this size," I said, gesturing at Godzilla's eighteen-inch mouth. "But I am willing to get into the Strike Zone with something a little more reasonable. All right, guys, let's bring in Junior."

Mario carried Junior over to me while Bob ushered Godzilla to the opposite side of his enclosure. I put a GoPro on my wrist, pointing straight up my left arm.

"That'll be the bite perspective," I said, looking down at the camera. Time was ticking down to the big event, and I was mentally preparing myself for what I was about to experience. As many

of you in the Coyote Pack know, I have a pretty high tolerance for pain, but that doesn't mean I don't feel every bit of it. I knew it was going to hurt like crazy when all of Junior's knifelike teeth sank into my skin.

I put my hands under Junior's scaly belly and neck, holding him just in front of my body. At this point, he was perfectly calm, but I still had to keep a good hold on him in case he had another burst of energy. His long tail drooped down by my side, from my hip to my knees.

"This is Junior," I said, turning his snout toward

YIKES!

Adult American alligators have a bite force of up to three thousand pounds per square inch!

the camera. "He's about three and a half feet in length, he weighs about twenty pounds, and he's only about two years old. The purpose of me getting chomped today by Junior is to prove that having an alligator as a pet is *not* a good idea."

This is Junior.

"Cut!" Mark called. I handed Junior off to Bob and crouched down into position. "All right, Coyote. You ready for this?" he asked.

I shut my eyes and breathed as deeply as I could, shaking off the nervousness that was starting to cloud my brain. With Junior in his hands, Bob knelt

down next to me, so that when I opened my eyes, I could see the gnarly teeth poking out over his jaw. I wanted to be ready, I *had* to be ready, but I don't think you're ever truly prepared for an alligator to sink his teeth into the meat of your forearm. I nodded to Mark; it was go time.

"Bob, you have a good hold on him?" I asked. Bob was holding

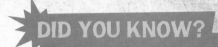
Junior at the neck—to keep his head from shaking—with his left arm supporting Junior's body. The alligator's back legs and tail were tucked under Bob's arm, which he could squeeze to keep the reptile from twisting into a barrel roll. Bob nodded, signaling he was set.

I'm about to enter the Strike Zone...

"All right, you guys ready?" I said, looking to Mark and Mario. They gave the thumbs-up.

"I'm Coyote Peterson, and I'm about to enter the Strike Zone with the American alligator." I scooted up, turned on the GoPro, and focused all my attention on Junior.

"Here we go..." I tapped the top of the alligator's nose, prompting him to slowly open his jaws,

revealing all those teeth. "One, two..."
Oh boy.

As I screamed *THREE!* in my head, I swung my arm away from my body and straight into his mouth. *CHOMP!* In a split second, Junior's jaws closed like a trap, and I could feel every single tooth digging into my skin.

"*ARRRRGH!*" At the top of my arm, I felt deep, heavy pressure from both sides of the alligator's head, but on the bottom, only one side of his jaw caught my flesh. I could tell he was trying to jerk his head, but Bob tightened his grip with both hands so Junior couldn't move a muscle.

"He's really holding on!" I grunted, squeezing air out of my pursed lips. *Good gravy! This is way worse than I thought!* My pulse was thundering through my veins like a herd of horses, and I felt a surge of adrenaline rush through my body. *Oh my gosh, deep breaths!*

CHOMP!

Mmmm!

"*MMMM!*" I growled. "That feels like..." I could barely think of the right words to say, it hurt so bad. "That feels like big needles going into my forearm." I looked down at my arm, pointed out the buried tips of his teeth, and felt another wave of pressure from his jaws. It seemed as if his grip was getting tighter and tighter. I was trying so hard to keep my focus, but all I could think was *IS HE EVER GOING TO LET GO?!*

"Coyote, remember this is about not keeping alligators as pets," prompted Mark. *Right! I knew that!* I nodded and looked back at his camera.

"An alligator of this size is certainly capable of giving you one really nasty bite." It was all I could muster. With my other hand, I pulled on the front of his jaws, trying to see if I could relieve some of the pressure.

"No, he's not letting go," I said, wincing as I tried to move my arm. "He's locked on to my arm, guys."

It's important to note at this point that we prepared for a lock-on situation like this. We had water, wood, and rubbing alcohol to use just in case, but I was really hoping we wouldn't need them all. Mario grabbed the bottle of water, unscrewed it, and handed it to me.

"*AHHHH!* There are some teeth underneath that have just popped through," I growled, grabbing the

bottle. I poured a bit of the water down over his nostrils. "*Ah, ah ah!*" Junior didn't like that. I tried to wriggle my arm free, thinking the alligator would let up, but Junior tightened his grip a bit—just as I said, "I hope he doesn't slide back...*ARGH!*"

He did. Now Junior's jaws were clamped down on a big chunk of muscle, and a few more teeth popped through my skin. *Oh geez oh geez oh geez.* My mind was blank, and it took all my focus to fight the urge to pull away from him. I was starting to regret this demonstration.

"He's biting down harder and harder and harder," I said. "I can't get him off. He's locked on there." I looked at Mark's face—which looked just as pale as my fingers—for some kind of support when Bob spoke up.

"Just a suggestion," he said gently. *Yes, please!* "Take this wood and put it here so he can't bite down any harder." He pointed to Junior's mouth just behind my arm. *That's right,* I thought. *The wood!*

I had nearly forgotten about the

wooden broom handle we had as a last resort. I grabbed the sturdy handle with my free hand and tried to position it properly, while moving as little as possible.

"This side," I said, lining the end of the broom handle up with the bite. I easily slid it though the small opening behind my arm and began rolling it back over each tooth in the alligator's mouth.

"*AH! Sst!*" I yelled, sucking air through my teeth. The broom handle wouldn't roll back any farther, but I could feel just a tiny bit of pressure release. *Just a little bit more, Coyote.* I wedged the handle up against the alligator's mouth and felt him struggle to keep ahold of me. *One last push,* I thought, *then I'll twist my*

arm out. With all my might, I jerked the wooden lever up, rolled my arm out, and pulled it away.

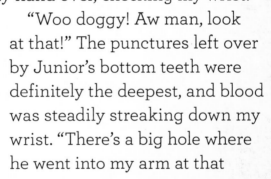

"*Oooh,*" I grumbled. "Wow. Thank you, Junior."

Looking down my arm, I could see purple indentations from his teeth that ran in a U shape on my skin. A few of the marks were starting to bleed as I flipped my hand over, checking my wrist.

"Woo doggy! Aw man, look at that!" The punctures left over by Junior's bottom teeth were definitely the deepest, and blood was steadily streaking down my wrist. "There's a big hole where he went into my arm at that

AMAZING!

Alligators often hold their breath underwater for around two hours at a time!

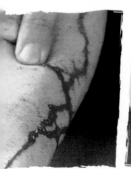
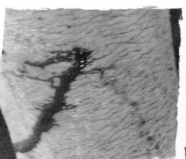

spot....It's the most uncomfortable sensation when you can feel a tooth pop through your skin....Mark, I need to stand up."

I walked away from the set and paced around, trying to block out the pain. My arms were shaking from the adrenaline, and I was finding it hard to describe what I was feeling. Mark walked over, asking if I was okay, and handed me a bottle of water. I gratefully gulped it down and concentrated on how to deliver a final message to the Coyote Pack.

On YouTube, the "Alligator Bite!" episode only showed about two minutes of what I went through, but Junior was latched on to me for over seven minutes! Frankly, I was lucky to walk away with only a few deep punctures and shallow cuts, but my arm was still at risk.

Due to the community of toxic bacteria between an alligator's teeth, the saliva in their mouth is almost like venom. Just one small puncture from the bite of an alligator can result in a rapid and dangerous infection, but the Brave Wilderness crew is always prepared for the consequences.

In making this episode, I was surrounded by a team of experts and had medical supplies on hand and a few emergency tools to use if the alligator didn't let go. Once we had finished filming, I spent at least an hour meticulously clearing debris, and then I thoroughly cleaned my arm with antibacterial wash, hydrogen peroxide, and antimicrobial ointment.

Can you imagine what could have happened if I didn't have any of those things?

Remember, Junior was only two years old, and Bob had a firm grip on him the whole time. What if he were *your* household pet? All it takes is half a second for an American alligator to whip their body around, open their jaws, and snap them down onto your arm. Even an alligator smaller than this can surge forward unexpectedly while you feed it or clean its cage... and if you were bitten, how would you get it off? How would you stop it from shaking its head or twisting into a death roll?

Just one moment of mishandling a reptile of this size would result in much worse injuries than what I sustained. After the bite, once I thoroughly cleaned and bandaged the damages, my arm developed deep bruises that I could feel down to the bone. It wasn't broken and I didn't need stitches, but it still took weeks for the punctures to fully heal.

Alligators may not be suitable as pets, but there are plenty of cool reptiles who are! Captive-bred lizards like bearded dragons or skinks are nonaggressive, family-safe pets who grow to a reasonable size and much prefer lettuce and crickets to human hands for dinner.

Tortoises, snakes, and frogs are also great options.

Even I have a tortoise named Green Bean who loves nothing

more than to mosey around his spacious enclosure, bask in the sun, or chow down on fresh lettuce.

I hope that by reading this chapter you realize that alligators are much better suited to life in the wild, being admired from a safe distance. They may look cute as eight-inch hatchlings at the pet store, but after just two years, they are big enough to inflict a bite that could send you to the hospital, or worse. It's always better to let wildlife experts like me take the pain instead of putting yourself in harm's way.

CHAPTER 5

CRUSHING
CRUSTACEANS

AMERICAN LOBSTER

FEAR	✦	✦	✦	✦	✦
IMPACT	✦	✦	✦	✦	✦
DAMAGE	✦	✦	✦	✦	✦
AFTERMATH	✦	✦	✦	✦	✦

TOTAL: 10/20

I've been pinched by many crustaceans over the course of my life. My worst pinches in childhood were by far the ones from crayfish, but my strongest pinch as an adult came from the Dungeness crab when I visited the fishing docks in Haines, Alaska. However, after releasing that episode on YouTube, I saw tons of comments pouring in about an entirely different crustacean: the American lobster.

Comments like *Coyote, have you ever been pinched by a lobster?! Would it break your hand?* Or even *I live in Maine, and my little brother got his toe broken from a wild lobster on the beach!* And at last: *Coyote, when are you going to do a lobster pinch?* They popped up all over the place, and when the Coyote Pack calls, Coyote Peterson answers. But before diving into another painful experience, I needed to do a little bit more research on these clawed creatures of the North Atlantic.

Although they have been caught as far south as North Carolina, American lobsters prefer marine temperatures between forty and sixty degrees Fahrenheit, which keeps them mostly contained between New York and northern Canada. They migrate up and down the coast, following tidal patterns by walking on the seafloor.

Lobsters are most active at night, preferring to hide in rocky crevasses during the day. They are both predators and scavengers and use highly developed sensory organs in their legs and antennae to find food in the dark. Their favorite finds include mollusks, fish, other crustaceans, and seaweed.

American lobsters are unique among

ONE SPECIES, MANY NAMES!

The species *Homarus americanus* (American lobster) is also known as Atlantic lobster, Canadian lobster, Maine lobster, New England lobster, northern lobster, true lobster, and Canadian reds!

all lobster species in North America because of their most iconic feature: their huge claws—or as they're technically called—

pincers. Other species of lobster, like spiny lobsters and rock lobsters, don't have large front pincers at all! What's most interesting about this standout feature is that each front claw is distinct. The crusher claw is used to break open the shells of mollusks and other crustaceans, while the ripper claw is used to tear food into bite-size pieces.

If I was going to get pinched by the American lobster, I wanted to experience the power of both claws. Would the crusher claw be strong enough to bruise the bones in my fingers? Would the ripper claw slice into my skin? Is one pinch worse than the other? These were all questions I wanted to answer, and the only way to find out was by experiencing that pinch for myself.

From everything my research provided, I thought that this would be the worst pinch of my life. I suppose I could have gone to my local seafood market to find an angry lobster to pinch me, but where's the fun in that? Venturing into an animal's habitat is a huge part of any Brave Wilderness episode, so to find the American lobster, there was only one place to go: Portland, Maine.

PORTLAND, MAINE

In June 2017, Mark, Mario, and I boarded a plane to Maine. (That rhymes!) Our plan was to meet one of the local lobster fishermen and charter a boat on open water, catch a good size lobster, and find out if the hype about the lobster's pinch was all it's cracked up to be.

We arrived at the docks in the early morning to meet the captain of our fishing vessel, Dave Laliberte. Dave is a seasoned lobsterman and has been sustainably catching lobsters on his trusty boat, the *Lucky Catch*, for over a decade. We motored away from the dock, through the Portland harbor, and out into the bay, heading for

YIKES!

American lobsters are more closely related to crayfish than they are to their spiny lobster cousins!

the buoys Dave had set the day before.

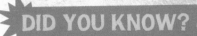
To catch lobster, most fishermen use lobster pots, which are special traps fitted with a lure and one-way entrance. Multiple lobster pots are secured to a rope, and each rope is tied to a buoy. When we reached the location of Dave's traps, we slowed our boat to a stop so that he could bring in the first batch.

As we reeled the trap in, I peered through the crisscrossed wire, hoping to see the silhouette of my target crustacean.

"Oh! We got a little one, but it's way too small. So, it's going to head back into the ocean. Bye, buddy!" I leaned over the side of the boat and plopped it back into the salty sea.

We brought up buoy after buoy, and emptied out pot after pot, but so far all the lobsters we managed to catch had to be released. Dave seemed unfazed, but I was expecting big lobsters left and right! We only had a few lines left to check, and just when it seemed like all was lost, we pulled up the lucky catch!

"Whoa, that one looks huge!" I said as the trap landed on the boat. "That could be the one!" I peered down into the netting, my eyes fixated on the monstrous claws of the crustacean

inside. I opened the hatch, slid my hand into the trap, and grabbed the hard shell of the big prize.

"That's over two pounds, I'd say!" Dave yelled from the front of the boat. I held the pincers up in front of me and couldn't believe my eyes.

"Look at those pinchers! I think this is it." I cheered, admiring the massive weaponry. Dave said it was probably the biggest lobster we'd get,

Those claws are huge!

which was a relief because I couldn't imagine getting pinched by anything bigger. The claws were as long as my fingers, and from what I could tell, as strong as a vice. *Oh boy, this guy could do some damage*, I thought. I carried it over to the holding tank and dropped it into the water. *See you later, buddy!*

After a successful day, we motored back into the harbor to unload the boat and prepare for the moment of truth. As soon as we made land, Mark, Mario, and I gathered our gear and prepared ourselves for what might be the worst, most painful, crushing pinch of my life. On the way to our location, our catch rested safely in a big bucket full of ocean water, which we would pour into a tank we had arranged beforehand. Since we were filming near the dock, I had only minutes before the agony of the almighty American lobster would surge through my hand.

As our car screeched to a halt, we quickly put everything in place before Mark and Mario, cameras in hand, got into position. Anxious to get started, I walked onto set.

"All right!" I said triumphantly to the cameras. "Now that we are in a controlled setting, we are about to get up close with the American lobster!"

I reached into the tepid water of the tank and grasped the lobster's carapace. As soon as it breached the surface, it furiously whacked my hand with its tail, flicking a salty spray across my face.

"Well, hello to you, too!" I jeered. "That's a defensive mechanism right there!" If it were in water, that motion would propel the lobster backward, and it would shoot out of my hand making a hasty escape. On land, however, it would only serve to startle a potential predator.

"Let's talk a little bit about the anatomy of this crustacean before we get into the pinch," I said. "The American lobster is the heaviest and longest-living crustacean in the world." In fact, lobsters are thought to be able to live anywhere from fifty to one hundred years in the wild and are able to get as heavy as forty pounds!

When lobsters hatch from eggs, they are tiny,

DID YOU KNOW?

A female lobster's tail is larger than a male's because they must have room to carry eggs. A one-pound female lobster can carry up to eight thousand eggs, while a nine-pound female can carry up to one hundred thousand!

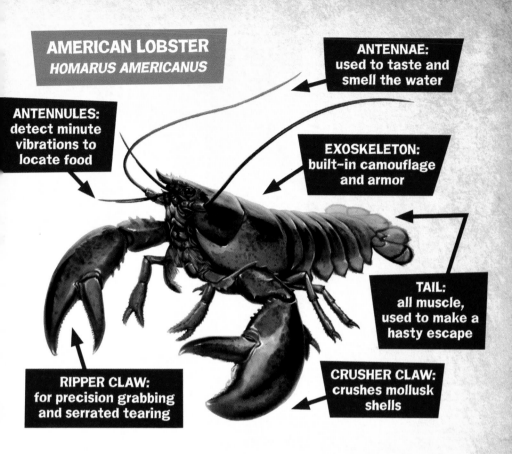

AMERICAN LOBSTER
HOMARUS AMERICANUS

ANTENNAE:
used to taste and
smell the water

ANTENNULES:
detect minute
vibrations to
locate food

EXOSKELETON:
built-in camouflage
and armor

TAIL:
all muscle,
used to make a
hasty escape

RIPPER CLAW:
for precision grabbing
and serrated tearing

CRUSHER CLAW:
crushes mollusk
shells

only about the size of a mosquito, and they are so light that they drift along at the water's surface. That means that throughout their long lives, they increase one hundred thousand times in size!

Now, you may be wondering, *Coyote, I thought lobsters were red!* Actually, lobsters are brownish green and orange with speckles of black and blue dotting their shells, which allows them to

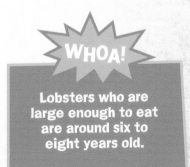

WHOA!

Lobsters who are
large enough to eat
are around six to
eight years old.

blend in perfectly with the sea floor. Lobsters only turn red when they are cooked. Luckily, the lobster I caught for this episode would be released back into the ocean and wouldn't end up on anyone's dinner plate!

"Now let's talk about the movement and body of this lobster. It's very similar to an insect, and technically lobsters are **arthropods**, so they're related to bugs!" Just like an insect, they have a head, thorax, and abdomen, and a hard exoskeleton instead of an inner skeleton.

HOW DO YOU SAY THAT?

Arthropods:
"AAR-thruh-pahds"

"Lobsters use their legs to slowly walk forward on the sea floor," I said. It's important to point out that lobsters have ten legs, including their claws, which are modified legs. "But if they sense a predator in their environment, they quickly shoot themselves

SWIMMERETS

backward using these flipper-like things called swimmerets." I dragged my finger across four pairs of swimmerets, which felt soft and flexible, and then pointed out the back of the tail, which is called the telson.

"Looks just like a whale tail," said Mario.

"It does! And their tails are incredibly strong; they're all muscle!" Turning to the cameras, I said, "If you guys are ready, it's time to get Lonnie"—the name I had given to the lobster—"out and see just how powerful both the crusher and ripper claws really are." I began mentally preparing myself for the pinch of a lifetime.

"Okay, Coyote," said Mark. "This is your final chance to call this off and save your hand."

"Nope!" I declared. "I'm going through with it! If there was ever a time to take a pinch from a giant lobster, this is it. You guys ready?" I looked at Mark, who had an expression of concern creasing his brow.

"I don't know, man. I get the feeling that this is a really bad idea." Mark seemed more worried than I was, but I was determined to complete this investigation not only for the Coyote Pack, but for my own curiosity. There was no turning back.

"Now, because these crustaceans lose a lot of their power out of water, this is going to have to happen immediately," I said. "I'm going to pick Lonnie up, gently set him down, and then *BOOM!*" I sliced my hand through the air showing that I was going pinkie-first into Lonnie's claw.

"I'm starting the countdown while he's still in the water, okay?" I confirmed.

"Okay," said Mark. "So, you're putting your left hand into the crusher claw first?"

DID YOU KNOW?

Lobsters have healing powers! They can regenerate their claws, legs, and antennae!

WEIRD!

Lobsters don't have tongues. Instead, they taste with sensory hairs on their legs that identify food!

I'm about to enter the Pinch Zone!

"Crusher claw first," I said. "Ripper claw second." Usually when I intentionally take a bite or sting, I have some degree of hesitation. This time, however, I wasn't slowing down to let creeping doubts cloud my mind. I was going full steam ahead and started the countdown.

"I'm Coyote Peterson, and I'm about to enter the Pinch Zone with the American lobster. One, two..." I grasped the monster American lobster by his back and held him out in front of me, shouting: "Three!"

I forced my hand in front of him, wedging it between the tip of his giant crusher claw, and took in a huge breath, bracing for impact. He flicked his tail defiantly, and my pinkie slipped around his wet pincer, so I moved the whole side of my hand into the danger zone of his viselike crusher. I gritted my teeth and squinted my eyes,

expecting the wave of pain to shock my system at any moment...any moment now...

Nothing. Lonnie wasn't pinching my hand at all. *Maybe if I jiggle my hand a bit...,* I thought, wriggling it around, but still nothing. *Well, that was anti-climactic.*

"Phooh." After all that anticipation, I felt like a deflated balloon. *What is going on?* A few seconds of silence ticked by, when Mark asked, "What's happening? Is he pinching?"

"He's not doing anything at all," I said bluntly. "Nothing at all, I'm completely all right." I guess it's not a *bad thing* that I wasn't going through terrible, crushing pain, but I was expecting *something* to happen!

"Maybe he likes you," suggested Mario.

I picked up Lonnie and set him back in his tank. "I thought this lobster was going to straight-up pinch me! Maybe I should try the ripper claw?" I pondered. "You guys ready for that?"

Mark gave the thumbs-up, so once again I started the countdown.

"I'm Coyote Peterson, and I'm about to

enter the Pinch Zone with the *ripper claw* of the American lobster!" I proclaimed, a little less enthusiastically. "One, two..." Again, I pulled the lobster out of the water, determined to inspire some kind of reaction. On *three*, I struck my right hand against the ripper claw, expecting it to open and strike out at me, delivering a painful blow.

Argh! I thought. This time, he wouldn't even open his claw! Frustrated, I set him down and delicately pried it apart. *Maybe my hand is too big?* I tried just my pinkie finger, getting it right between those pinchy points on the end of the claw.

YIKES!

The American lobster's claws are actually modified legs, called great chelipeds.

Sigh! Come on, Lonnie! But still, nothing.

"He has absolutely no interest in pinching me," I conceded, setting him back into the water. "This is not going according to plan." *Something's not right here*, I thought. *We need to rethink this.*

149

We had set out to experience the strength of a lobster pinch, but so far it was more of a firm squeeze. Maybe the powerful pinch was just a myth! After hearing stories about broken hands and crushed fingers, I was pretty disappointed when my own experience lacked any sort of pressure or puncture at all. If those stories had any truth to them, we had to figure out how to entice a stronger reaction from our scuttling friend.

"Coyote, lobsters are nocturnal," said Mario. "Maybe we should try again tonight."

Following Mario's advice, we cleaned up our scene, refreshed our lobster with new salty water, and found a better location for filming once it was dark. After thinking about lobsters' preferred environments, we decided to wait until it was cool enough that we could see our breath. Hours later, it was time to give Lonnie one more shot at inflicting his strongest pinch.

When we got started, it was about eleven o'clock at night. Wasting no time, I got in front of the cameras, picked him out of the water, and set

FLICK FLICK FLICK!

my hand in front of him once again.

"*Annnnd* pinch me!" I said, touching his claws with my hand. *FLICK, FLICK, FLICK,* he whacked me with his powerful tail. "Nothing. He's immediately just thinking flight." I gently set him down and racked my brain for any detail I might be missing.

"Part of me wonders if maybe these claws are so big that when he's out of the water, he's not even

Friendly neighborhood lobster

capable of holding them up." I picked up his ripper claw and held it to my hand. "But even when he's down like this, he's just not interested in pinching."

"I think Lonnie's too nice." Mark laughed. *Maybe he's right,* I thought.

"I think we have busted the myth," I declared. "I don't think lobsters have a very powerful pinch."

"I have one more idea," said Mark. "I think what we have here is a friendly lobster, and what we need are *angry* lobsters. If I were a lobster, you know what would make me angry? Being at a lobster restaurant."

"You think they know we're not going to harm them?" I asked, gently holding Lonnie under his legs. "I mean, we are in Maine and there are lobster restaurants everywhere. Maybe we should get one of those lobsters, save it from getting cooked, and see if it will pinch me."

"Yeah, let's go find ourselves an angry lobster!" Mark replied.

The next morning, we headed straight for a local lobster restaurant. The owner of Estes Lobster House must have thought we were joking when we asked, "Do you guys have angry lobsters here?" Much to our surprise however, she said, "You betcha!" After we explained that we were trying to prove the power of the pinch, she generously offered her restaurant as our next location for filming.

We walked into the tank room of the restaurant and marveled at the enormous pool that sat in the middle of it. Fresh, chilly ocean water was pumped into the basin, and the room was mostly

kept dark, even during the day. It seemed
that the conditions were right, and these lobsters
hadn't been handled by gentle humans in days like
Lonnie had.

"This trough is filled with fresh lobsters!" I said
cheerfully. "Guess we'll see if any of them are angry!"
I reached into the water and examined a few of the
candidates, looking for the largest and grumpiest
lobster I could find.

"These are all market-size lobsters, which means
they are all between one and a half to two pounds," I
said. I brought one of the potential pinchers out and
looked over its claws carefully. All the lobsters had
rubber bands on them, which kept the crustaceans
from harming one another while in the tank.

"That's a whopper of a claw right there!" I said,
holding a feisty lobster up to the camera. "Look how
it hooks over; it might actually break skin." I didn't

need to look any further. As soon as I peeled off the rubber band, the lobster immediately opened its crusher claw defensively.

"All right, guys, I'm going to dip him in the water, bring him up, and then, *WHACK*, put my hand in there. You ready?" I said to Mark and Mario, who gave the usual thumbs-up. *PLOP!* I dipped it back into the tank, took a deep breath, and delivered my signature line to the Coyote Pack:

Oh boy, here we go!

"I'm Coyote Peterson, and I'm about to enter the Pinch Zone with the American lobster. Ready? One, two..." I lifted the lobster up, took one last quick gasp of air, and at last said: "Three!" The angry arthropod waved his claws in the air threateningly as I offered the edge of my hand to his crusher claw. *CRUNCH!*

"*Arrghhhh!*" I screamed, taken off guard at his immense strength. "Ah-ah-ah! Wow, it's actually worse this time!" I'd expected this lobster to be a dud, just like Lonnie, but holy mackerel, it really packed a

WHACK!

CRUNCH!

punch. It felt like my hand was being ground between a mouth full of molars, and instead of letting up, the pressure only got tighter.

"*Huuurgh!* That's a lot worse than yesterday!" I exclaimed, clenching my teeth. My pulse went into hyperdrive, and I could feel my heart racing inside my chest. I felt little to no anticipation before the pinch, but I was now experiencing more agony than any crustacean had delivered before, and my mind was buzzing with overwhelming shock. *Let go, let go, LET GO!*

After about ten seconds, I'd had enough, and I wriggled my hand free, knocking my hand bones against the tough ridges of the crusher claw. *Ah-ah-argh!* That's what I get for underestimating an angry lobster!

That's a lot worse than yesterday!

155

"Did he get you?" chuckled Mario.

"Oh yeah! He got me good!" I gasped, turning my painful hand over. "That is a *huge* difference from yesterday. Ah man!" I moved my fingers slowly, feeling every muscle struggle with pain from the impact. My bones weren't broken, and he didn't break skin, but I still had one more claw left to try.

"Let's try the ripper claw," I said, pulling the second rubber band off his pincer. "You ready?" Afraid I'd lose my nerve, I didn't even bother to switch hands. I gave a hasty countdown and quickly sliced my hand into the lobsters gapping ripper claw. *WHAM!*

"*AH!*" I shouted as I felt the serrated points digging in. "*Arrrgh!* Wow, that's a lot sharper!" It felt like tiny teeth were grating against my skin, and I couldn't stop my hand from shaking as the lobster increased its pressure. *Yah-oh-hah-argh!* I couldn't even move my fingers as I tried to pry him away with my left hand, still clinging onto his carapace.

"That ripper claw is just locked onto my hand!" I grunted. "This is one hundred percent different from the lobster yesterday." The ridges of the ripper claw felt like dull saw blades, but the worst part was the very tip, which had two interlocking daggerlike points. With every slight movement, I could feel those sharp spikes dig deeper between the bones of my hand.

"*Ssst!* Ahck!" I gasped. "This is a lot sharper than the Dungeness crab—and it keeps locking on harder!" *Geez, aren't you tired yet?!* I silently begged the lobster to release me. I wasn't sure how I was going to get my hand out without losing some skin, so I did the only thing I could think of.

"Maybe if I dip it in the water, it'll let go?" I considered, feeling another twinge of sharp pressure

jolt up my arm. I wasn't sure if the lobster had broken skin, but it felt like he was hitting a nerve.

"Those serrated edges are digging into the back of my hand," I said, starting to panic. "I'm trying to pull it out, but it is locked in there! I'm going to have to dunk it in the water." Without further debate, I plunged my hands into the salty tank, completely submerging the crustacean.

"Let go, let go," I mumbled. "*Ahh!* He's pinching down harder!" With one final twist of my wrist, I wrenched my hand free of the sharp, serrated ripper claw and flung myself back away from the murky tank before me.

"*Ahhh-ha-ha-ha,*" I growled, hastily scooping the lobster back out of the water. "Yikes! That was a huge difference! Look at the impressions in my hand." In two painful, dotted lines, deep indentations streaked across the palm and back of my hand, which was

still shaking. I could see purple blood blisters pooling under my skin, and my muscles ached with every shift of my fingers.

"I can feel my hand starting to swell," I remarked, wincing. "I'd say that was successful. It was much more powerful than the lobster yesterday, but a lobster of this size was not capable of breaking skin, let alone breaking bone. I'd have to say, though, it was definitely worse than the Dungeness crab!"

Mark, Mario, and I may have busted the bone-breaking myth, but one question still remained: *Why did this lobster pinch so much harder than Lonnie?* My

assumption was that the fresh ocean water being pumped into the restaurant was significantly colder than the water we had in the tanks the day before, and

the tank room was pitch-black (until we'd come in and starting filming), mimicking the lobsters' natural environment. Couple that with being surrounded by other angry lobsters, and you have a perfect storm of aggression.

"In the back of his mind, this lobster may know that he and all of his friends could end up on a dinner plate!" I laughed. "But the good news for this lobster is that we are going to purchase and release it back out into the wild!"

If I could save every lobster from a dinner plate, believe me, I would. It's important to know that while lobster fishing may seem cruel, it's a practice done with the utmost care and respect for these incredible creatures. Lobster fishermen and women like Dave are conservationists first and adhere to the strict regulations of lobster fishing to preserve the species—and their own livelihoods—for generations to come.

   After two long days of trial and error, Mark, Mario, and I finally found the answers we were looking for. Finding, catching, and handling wild American lobsters took a lot more effort than we anticipated, and to our surprise no amount of coaxing could incite our friendly lobster, Lonnie, to deliver a mind-numbing pinch. Even for Coyote Peterson, things don't always go as planned, but with persistence, curiosity, and out-of-the-box thinking, we finally reached our conclusion.

   In the dark, chilly water of their natural environment, American lobsters are at their best, and are most likely to deliver a full-strength, painful pinch with their two enormous

claws. Once they're handled and they warm up, however, they become much more docile, focusing on flight rather than fight.

If I had to rank the two distinct claws against one another, I'd have to say that the sharp spines and serrated teeth of the ripper claw take the cake. The deep impressions left behind on my hand lasted only for a few hours, but the swelling and blood blisters remained for several days. Since neither pincer was able to break skin, a quick wash-up was all I needed, but for weeks, my right hand was sore and stiff from all the pressure on my bones, muscles, and nerves.

The lobsters we worked with were all less than three pounds. They may be capable of breaking mussel shells with their crusher claw and tearing meat with their ripper claw, but I can officially say that at that size they aren't strong enough to break an *adult* human hand. I don't recommend putting *yourself* on the sharp end of those claws, though,

as it is definitely the strongest, most painful crustacean grip I have ever experienced.

After filming was done and we had made our live-lobster purchase, Mark, Mario, and I set out once again for the shores of Portland, Maine, to say goodbye to our feisty crustacean friends. Large Lonnie and our new friend, Angry Andy, happily made their way back out to their deep-water homes as I waved from the sandy beach of the harbor, saying:

"I'm Coyote Peterson. Be Brave...Stay Wild—we'll see ya on the next adventure!"

CHAPTER 6

TINY TEETH, TERRIBLE TEMPER!

TOKAY GECKO

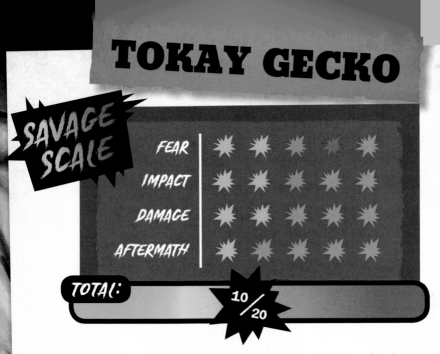

SAVAGE SCALE

FEAR	✷	✷	✷	✷	✷
IMPACT	✷	✷	✷	✷	✷
DAMAGE	✷	✷	✷	✷	✷
AFTERMATH	✷	✷	✷	✷	✷

TOTAL: 10/20

In the spring of 2018, Mark, Mario, and I had a busy week of production at one of our favorite locations: Homestead, Florida. For our stay, we chose a big lodge surrounded by an agricultural grove, accessible by a long, winding driveway lined by row after row of lemon, almond, and orange trees. As we entered the quiet, tree-lined drive, the sun slipped under the horizon, blanketing our arrival with a quiet darkness.

As we unloaded the car by flashlight, all we could hear was the soft hum of frogs singing in the distance and the shuffle of our footsteps as we carried our gear into the house. As I grabbed my bags and started making my way to the door, an unfamiliar sound suddenly rang out.

To-kay!

What was that?! I thought, stopping dead in my tracks.

To-KAY!

I dropped the luggage and whirled around, locking eyes with Mario behind me. "Is that you, Mario?" I whispered.

"Is what me?" he asked, looking confused. As he started to walk over, I heard it again—To-KAY!—and put out one hand to stop his footsteps. TO-KAY!

"You don't hear that?!" I hissed. Mark, who was inside the house, hurried out to us with an excited look on his face.

"Guys, something's near the house. Did you hear that?" he murmured. Slowly, we crept toward the warm light of the porch, our eyes darting from the roof to the walls, searching for the noisy critter nearby.

TO-KAY! it sang again, and Mario's face lit up.

"I think...I think it's a tokay gecko!" he said cautiously. "I've heard that they've been introduced to this area, but I've never seen them here before."

MRRAAH, TO-KAY!

No way, I thought. *Tokay geckos live*

FUN FACT!

Tokay geckos get their name from their unique barking, which sounds like *to-KAY!* Their scientific name is *Gekko gecko*, which is also imitative of the sounds that they make.

in Indonesia and India...but that sure sounds like one.

TSK-TSU-TSU-RN-RN-RN! it growled. TO-KAY!

"I think you're right, Mario!" I said as the sound grew louder. Just then, we heard another call in the distance, To-kay, and then a third To-KAY! and then a fourth from just around the corner...TO-KAY!

"Coyote, I found it!" hissed Mark. "It's on the wall!" Mark's flashlight had just illuminated its target when, suddenly, the big blue gecko darted away from view, hiding in the shadow of some plants nearby.

HOMESTEAD, FLORIDA

As it turned out, this particular area was home to several foreign invaders, and the tokay gecko was definitely one of them. These stunning, noisy reptiles were brought to the United States through the pet trade and were unfortunately released into Florida's ecosystem after the people who bought them could no longer care for them.

The natural range of the tokay gecko spans throughout the rich tropical areas of Southeast Asia, with populations spreading through India, the Philippines, and Indonesia. Since they are primarily arboreal, tokay geckos have adapted to human habitation and traverse upright walls, ceilings, roofs, and rafters with ease. These big geckos are primarily insectivores, but due to their size, they are capable of hunting anything from baby birds and rodents to other reptiles.

Their adaptability and opportunistic behavior allow the tokay gecko to thrive in any warm tropical climate, and they have now established populations in Florida, Hawaii, and the Caribbean. In their native habitats, geckos have few predators once they reach adulthood. In non-native areas, they have almost no predators at all, leaving them unchecked and able to grow populations in the hundreds in just a few years.

After an exciting night, Mark, Mario, and I decided that we had to feature these striking geckos in an episode. It just so happened that we traveled to Florida in search of other invasive reptiles—the amazing veiled chameleon and the massive Burmese python—so adding another to the list seemed like fate. Aside from their cool appearance and unique bark, there was something else about the tokay gecko that interested *me* in particular: the tokay gecko's bite.

As a mainstay in the pet trade for several decades, tokay geckos have earned themselves quite the reputation as the bulldogs of the lizard world. During my childhood, I'd heard various rumors and stories warning that when a tokay latches on with its tiny sharp teeth, it won't let go. These feisty creatures are said to be one of the most aggressive small lizards you could have as a pet, and often choose *fight* rather than *flight*.

Now, you may be saying, *Coyote, come on. It's just a gecko—how bad could it be?* Well, I'd always wondered if the rumors were true, and this was my chance to finally find the answer for myself. Once I had safely caught one of these noisy lizards and displayed its amazing features to the Coyote Pack, I'd have

the chance to determine once and for all: Is the tokay gecko's bite as bad as its bark?

First, I had to catch one!

As an arboreal species, tokay geckos primarily live in trees. Most gecko species are equipped with super-grippy pads on their feet, giving them an unrivaled ability to climb on any surface! Since they only come out at night, I would need the help of both Mark and Mario to make the catch, and as I would soon discover, that was easier said than done.

We had only been in Homestead for two nights when we decided to start our search, and we patiently waited on the porch for the sun to drop below the horizon. As a few stars began to sparkle in the dark sky above, we heard that signature call ring out from the thick grove of trees around us: To-kay!

> **FUN FACT!**
>
> Not all geckos are good climbers. Some species of terrestrial geckos don't have sticky pads on their toes at all!

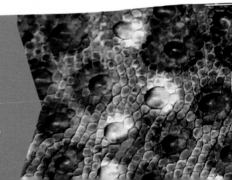

> **DID YOU KNOW?**
> The bright coloration on the tokay gecko actually gives them incredible camouflage. That's because they can lighten or darken their skin to blend into their surroundings!

"Did you hear that?" whispered Mario. I nodded silently and scanned the branches with my flashlight as we began searching the property around our rental house. In addition to the geckos, the insects were out in full force, and a light din of fluttering wings and chirping crickets could be heard in all directions.

"Where there are bugs, there should be lizards," I said hopefully, squinting my eyes. "What I'm doing is searching for eyeshine. The gecko's eyes will reflect the light from my flashlight and spark out against the darkness." I held my light up to my nose and pointed the beam into the environment straight in front of my eyes.

"A good place to start looking is near any little crevice in the trunks of these trees." As the beam from the flashlight ran up and down, from trunk to trunk, I caught the bright glow of eyeshine bouncing back at me. To-KAY, it barked.

"*Psst!* Mark, Mario!" I hissed, my eyes on the prize. The gecko was immediately onto me, however, and just as I moved in for the catch, it quickly bolted down a nearby hollow in the bark of the tree, concealing itself in darkness.

"Argh! As soon as it heard my footsteps coming, it was gone!" I sighed. "Man, they are quick! I thought it went down the side of this tree, but it managed to squeeze itself down this little crevice. Let's keep searching." I shined my flashlight down into the hollow, but there was no sign of the lizard at all. *On to the next tree*, I thought, crunching through the leaf litter.

"Here we go, right there!" I said, immediately rushing forward. *"Arrgh!"* I flung my arm around the back of the tree trunk where I saw the critter dart off, but again there was no sign of it.

"Did you get it?" asked Mario, approaching behind me. I reached up the trunk as high as I could and even started climbing up the tree's base to inspect the shadowy places above.

"Nope. Argh! There's a hole right here!" I grumbled. "He just went down into the hole of that tree." That was the fourth miss of the night, and I could feel myself getting frustrated.

As I continued to search, every time I illuminated a gecko's eyes and started to move in, they would either skitter up the tree to the highest branches or shimmy down a tight crevice, out of sight and out of reach. I clambered up

after them, but one by one, they made their hasty escape. Still, I wasn't giving up.

My persistence led us deeper into the grove, and every footfall announced our presence with a loud *CRUNCH* of the leaves under our feet. The beam from my light bounced on every reachable branch, trunk, and twig, and I was determined to catch one of these camouflaged critters by surprise.

"Eyeshine right on the side of that tree!" I said. "Mark, do you see it?" The gecko quickly shifted his body out of sight, but I could still see his tail poking out from the back of the trunk, giving away his position. Neither Mark nor Mario could spot the elusive lizard with their cameras, but I wasn't letting this one get away.

Got him!

"I'm just going to go for it!" I said, crouching low and out of the gecko's line of sight. Keeping myself hidden from view, I sprang into action, reaching with the full length of my arms and legs, and wrapping my hand around the back of the timber to the exact spot the tokay gecko was perched. *Yes! Bull's-eye!*

"I got him! Woo! He's already trying to bite me," I yelled. "That is about as good a grab as I could possibly make! Let me slowly peel this guy up and off of the tree...." The gecko's toes were clinging on to the rough edges of the tree's bark, so I slid my other hand under his feet to pry them free, and then I hopped down off the trunk.

"There we go!" I said, sticking my landing in the leaves. "He is all chompy, trying to get my fingers in his mouth!" From the moment I caught him, the gecko's mouth was wide open, defensively displaying his row of tiny teeth and deep-purple and red throat. He jerked his head side

to side, almost daring me to get my fingers closer.

Finally, after a long night of searching and several unsuccessful attempts, I had managed to catch a tokay gecko! I knew this one was a male, because males are larger than females and this individual was pretty

big. His skin felt velvety soft in my hands, and as I crouched down in front of the cameras, I could hear him emitting cranky little grumbles and squeaks in protest.

MRRAH!

"Wow!" I marveled. "Look at the coloration!" I ran my finger down his back, pointing out the light-blue and copper speckling dotting his gray-blue skin. Mrrah! he squeaked, making a feeble grab at my hand.

"Oh, I hear you!" I said. "That bark is what we've been hearing all night. It's a defensive warning that *If you get your finger close, I'm going to give you one very painful chomp!*" I shifted his head toward the camera, showing off his colorful mouth. "It's almost aposematic in design, with black and bright red."

Usually, **aposematic** coloration is found on venomous or poisonous creatures, serving as a warning to potential predators: *Don't eat me—I'm dangerous.* Tokay geckos are not venomous, but their mouths are armed with razor-sharp teeth and powerful jaws and can give potential predators or interested handlers a surprisingly nasty bite. Raahh!

HOW DO YOU SAY THAT?

Aposematic:
"AP-oh-so-MA-tik"

ARRH.

"Whoa!" I cried, startled by the gecko's quick grab at my finger. "Whoa, buddy. He's going at me, trying to get a bite going." Arrh!

Ooh, too close to my finger!

he barked again as he turned his body and craned his neck, getting his teeth close to my fingers. I was now using both hands just to keep my hold on him, careful not to squeeze his little tail.

Like most gecko species, tokay geckos are equipped with a clever defense mechanism called **caudal autotomy**. When caught by a predator, they can sever a section of their tails, distracting the hunter and giving themselves the chance to make a hasty escape. Fortunately, the tail isn't gone forever. Over a matter of weeks, a new tail will grow in its place, but

HOW DO YOU SAY THAT?

Caudal:
"CAW-dull" (meaning tail)

Autotomy:
"uh-TOT-oh-mee"

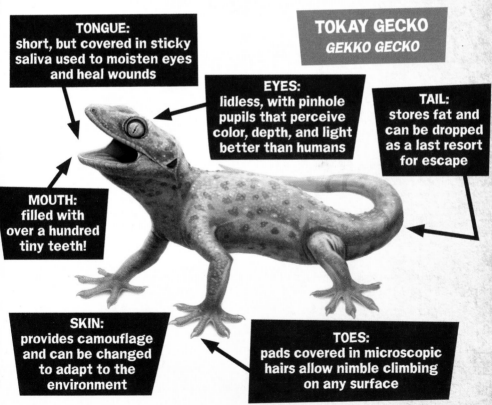

TONGUE:
short, but covered in sticky saliva used to moisten eyes and heal wounds

TOKAY GECKO
GEKKO GECKO

EYES:
lidless, with pinhole pupils that perceive color, depth, and light better than humans

TAIL:
stores fat and can be dropped as a last resort for escape

MOUTH:
filled with over a hundred tiny teeth!

SKIN:
provides camouflage and can be changed to adapt to the environment

TOES:
pads covered in microscopic hairs allow nimble climbing on any surface

it will never be as long as the original.

"That came out of nowhere!" said Mark.

The feisty gecko continued to twist around in my hand, trying to reach back at my fingers.

"Yeah, they are incredibly aggressive!" I said, looking down at his bright-yellow eyes. "They will explode into action. The males are more aggressive than females and are very territorial. There's a chance that this tree right here is this little Godzilla's domain. Hopefully, I can get him to calm down a little bit. I don't want to take a bite...yet."

As I readjusted my grasp, I felt the gecko's constant gaze follow my every move. Tokay geckos have incredible eyesight both at night and during the day. Their unique pupils filter light through a series of pinholes, giving them an incredible sense of depth perception in both low light and daylight. Since they

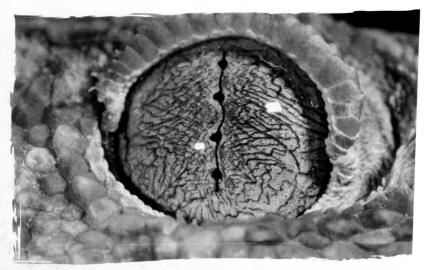

are ambush predators, this keen sense of distance is essential for them to take quick action when hunting their prey.

"These geckos are voracious predators," I continued, "and will eat pretty much anything they can fit into their mouths. That includes insects, baby birds, and small or young mammals. Even other lizards are fair game for this predator." Like many reptiles, tokay geckos crush their food and swallow it whole. For their size, they have very strong jaws, allowing them to reduce the size of their meal into one manageable gulp.

"Now let's look at one of the hallmark traits of this gecko: its feet," I said. "These toes are all covered with sticky pads and end in sharp claws. It's this combination that allows them to climb over any surface, including glass." I say *sticky pads*, but actually each pad is covered in thousands of microscopic hairs! The only thing a gecko has trouble

DID YOU KNOW?

The amazing microscopic hairs on a gecko's toes are called setae, and each hair branches off into hundreds of smaller bristles called spatulae. Even the gecko's hairs have hairs!

sticking to is a wet surface or Teflon (like the pots and pans in your kitchen!).

"Now, the tokay gecko has long been one of my favorite lizard species," I said, "and when I was a kid, just ten years old, I wanted one as a pet more than anything." Let me tell you the full story.

It was a brisk fall afternoon when I stumbled upon a picture of the tokay gecko for the first time. Featured on the cover of a new issue of *Reptiles* magazine, its bright-yellow eyes and stunning coloration seized my attention, and I promptly checked out the magazine from the library.

YIKES!

Tokay geckos can have up to a hundred tiny teeth in their mouths at a time!

Later that evening, my mom and I stopped at our local pet store for some dog food, and just as I had done countless times, I wandered over to the reptile and amphibian enclosures. There, hiding behind a few plastic plants, was the tokay gecko. It was meant to be! I beckoned my mom over and excitedly pointed it out, begging her to let me get one. "If you get straight As on your report card and save your allowance, you can get one," she said.

Boy, did I work hard! Not only did I

dedicate myself to my studies, but I mowed every neighbor's lawn, pulled every weed, and washed every car to earn enough for my new favorite reptile. After a few weeks, I went back to the pet store ready to take home my very own tokay gecko.

I was over the moon and felt an overwhelming sense of pride for all my hard work leading up to my well-earned reptilian reward. Just as we were about to check out, however, the guy at the register said, "Are you sure? This is an aggressive lizard. They have an incredibly painful bite and hold on like a bulldog." *Whatever, man*, I thought, *I'm tough!* "Also, they bark like crazy at night." *I can sleep through anything!* "Oh, and you have to feed it a lot of baby mice." *Oh.*

My mom absolutely refused to let me take home a tokay, saying that they weren't safe pets and that she would never feed live mice to any reptile. I will never forget the crushing disappointment and heartbreak I felt walking through the door empty-handed. Just a short conversation with some guy at the pet store, and all my hard work was for nothing.

"Now, looking back on it in hindsight, my mom was probably right," I said, looking at the wildly feisty gecko still clutched in my hands. "I'm sure a lot of you guys think, *This is such a cool lizard—I want one, too!* Honestly, unless you have the means and experience to care for it, the tokay gecko is *not* a good pet." What I mean by *the means* is, these lizards eat constantly, and—as I witnessed firsthand—make loud vocalizations all night long.

WEIRD!

Most gecko species, including the tokay gecko, don't have eyelids. Instead, they have modified, transparent scales covering each eye, and must lick their eyes with their tongues to clear away dirt and debris!

That's probably why they ended up living out here in Florida. Someone, unaware of their needs and aggressive attitude, likely released these geckos after discovering that they were too much to handle.

That was a long story, now back to the bite! As someone who has taken intentional bites and stings from a variety of creatures, I was still skeptical of just how bad a bite from the tokay gecko really was.

"I'm pretty curious," I said. "I've

been bitten by many lizard species, but never the tokay gecko. If I was still ten years old, would it really do that much damage? I think we better try it out."

"Are you seriously going to do this?" asked Mark. Since we didn't plan on finding these foreign invaders in Florida at all, we hadn't prepared for a bite episode, either. Luckily, we always carry first-aid kits in our backpacks for every adventure, so my safety was not at risk.

"I'm going to do it," I said confidently. "I gotta see how painful it is! Are they truly the bulldog of the gecko kingdom? Or is it going to bite and quickly let go?" **Mrrah**, squeaked the gecko, as if chiming in. *I guess you're ready for the bite*, I thought.

"It's time to enter the Bite Zone!" I declared. Holding the gecko in my right hand, I brought the pointer finger of my left hand up to his face, just out of reach from his jaws.

"In case he doesn't let go, I have a contingency plan," I explained. "I'll set the lizard down, let go of his body, and see if he'll release my finger. If not,

WHOA!

In addition to being able to drop their tails, geckos also store fat in their tails! When food becomes scarce, they can draw on this fat as a resource until food becomes plentiful.

I'll have a reptile locked onto one of my fingers for the rest of the scene! You guys ready?" Taking a deep breath, I took one last look at the gecko's mouth, then

my finger, as I prepared to take the full brunt of those sharp teeth.

"I'm Coyote Peterson, and I'm about to enter the Bite Zone with the tokay gecko," I said, stroking the back of its head. "One...two...three!" *CHOMP!*

As though I flipped the trigger of a mousetrap, the gecko's jaws slammed shut on my finger with more force and pain than I expected. It felt like I'd

slammed my finger in a drawer—if the drawer was lined with forty tiny needles—and I have to admit I was completely taken by surprise.

"*Arrgh!*" I screamed. "*Ooh!* Yargh!" He ground his jaws back and forth, sliding his sharp teeth farther into my finger, like an extra dose of punishment. In just a few seconds, however, it was over. He jerked his head away, licked his lips, and then resumed his threatening display.

"*Ahh!*" I said, relieved. "Hah! A bite and let-go!" *Take that, pet-store man.*

"Ugh, go ahead and zoom in on my finger there," I said to Mario, holding it up in front of my face. From front to back, small lacerations and punctures dotted my digit, which was covered in little specks of blood.

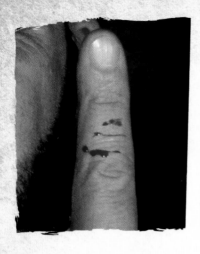

"Why did you do that?" Mark asked, shaking his head.

"I had to know how bad it was!" I insisted. "And honestly, guys, I have to say *thanks* to my mom. If I were a kid, I can't imagine how much worse it could have been if this creature latched onto my little fingers."

Even though the gecko let go of me, it was still able to do a surprising amount of damage in the few seconds it had its grip...and I have to say, it was far more painful than I expected!

***

Because tokay geckos are invasive in Florida, we couldn't let our feisty friend back onto his tree.

Instead, for further research and educational efforts, he was donated to a local wildlife facility, where he is an ambassador for his species.

Invasive reptiles like the tokay gecko pose a danger to

the South Florida ecosystem and native wildlife where they are introduced.

Since they're not normal prey items themselves, their population is able to grow unchecked, putting further strain on the wide food web they consume. Native animals like birds, rodents, lizards, and insects have struck an important balance in their habitats. Introducing non-native predators not only affect the prey populations, but the plants and insects they eat, the predators who eat them, and the natural landscape they live in.

While I understand the temptation to get a tokay gecko as an imported pet,

WHOA!

Since they are nocturnal, tokay geckos bark mostly at night, and especially during the mating season. It's estimated that their bark and clicking sounds can be heard from over a hundred yards away.

it's best to leave them in the tropical Southeast Asian habitat they call home. If you have your heart set on a lizard as a pet, fear not! Captive-bred bearded dragons and leopard geckos make excellent family companions. Not only are they docile and even-tempered, but they're also insectivores, meaning no baby mice have to be harmed for their feeding. Unfortunately for South Florida, invasive reptiles are likely there to stay. The tokay gecko, Burmese python, Argentine tegu, and veiled chameleon are just a few of the exotic animals who have been imported through the pet trade. All it takes is two individuals, the right environmental conditions, and plenty of food for exotic pets to establish themselves.

TO-KAY!

Meeting a wild tokay gecko was the last thing I would have expected on my journey to Homestead. But when the opportunity to get up close with one of the most beautiful, feisty, and unique lizards presented itself, I knew it would be an encounter I would never forget. I guess you could say that my curiosity got the best of me, but now that I've experienced the aggression and painful bite of this creature, I can say with confidence that I'm glad I didn't get one as a kid.

CHAPTER 7

MISTAKEN FOR A MOCCASIN

NORTHERN WATER SNAKE

SAVAGE SCALE

FEAR	✹ ✹ ✹ ✹ ✹
IMPACT	✹ ✹ ✹
DAMAGE	✹ ✹ ✹ ✹
AFTERMATH	✹ ✹ ✹ ✹

BECAUSE OF CONTINUED BLEEDING

TOTAL: 9/20

As the frost and snow melt away and flowers break ground with the coming spring, people from all over the eastern United States take to the outdoors to welcome the warm weather, but they're not the only ones. Slowly roused from their deep slumber, slithering, scaly serpents also emerge from hibernation. Even though a dangerous encounter with these reptiles is rare, these legless residents give many of us humans the creeps.

The most common reported fear, or phobia, across the world is ophidiophobia: the fear of snakes. Whether they are venomous or nonvenomous, terrestrial or aquatic, big or small, about a third of the world population report having some kind of aversion to these streamlined reptiles, and even go so far as to banish them from their natural environments. Part of my mission as a wildlife educator and enthusiast is to alleviate that fear.

One of the most difficult obstacles to overcome in that mission is reversing the belief that all snakes are potentially deadly. Of the more than thirty-four hundred snake species throughout the world, fewer

CORAL SNAKE – ELAPID

than three hundred are venomous. Of those, less than half are capable of delivering a potentially fatal bite. The United States is home to twenty recognized venomous snake species, all of which are either **elapids** or pit vipers.

That's some fancy technical language, so let me explain. Elapids are venomous snakes who are found all across the world and include species like coral snakes, sea snakes, and cobras. Their body structure is typically long and slender, and like nonvenomous snakes, they have round pupils, oval-shaped heads, and fixed teeth. Pit vipers, on the other hand, are in the viper

family and differ in that they have heat-sensing pits between their eyes and nostrils. They have triangular-shaped heads, thick bodies, vertical pupils, and hinged, flexible fangs that fold back against the roof of their closed mouths.

Venomous snakes, while potentially dangerous, are much less common than their nonvenomous counterparts. In North America, there are over one hundred recognized species of nonvenomous snakes called **colubrids**. Colubrids are described as "typical snakes." They live on every continent across the world except Antarctica and thrive in every biome available in the United States except Alaska.

Colubrids are the most common of all snakes and include species like the garter snake, king snake, and water snake. No matter where you live, I'm sure you've seen their long smooth bodies, oval-

HOW DO YOU SAY THAT?

Elapid:
"EL-uh-pid" or "EE-la-pid"

Colubrid:
"KOL-uh-brid" or "kuh-LOO-brid"

YIKES!

Pit vipers have hollow fangs, which they use to inject their toxic venom into prey when they bite!

shaped heads, and camouflaged scales as they lurk in your garden, bask near bodies of water, or hunt in your local park. Unfortunately, these relatively harmless reptiles are frequently misidentified and villainized as venomous because they often resemble and mimic behaviors of their toxic cousins. One species most famous for this misguided mix-up is the northern water snake.

If you live in Ohio like I do, the northern water snake is probably a reptile you have seen before. In fact, this species' range covers every state in the Northeast and even stretches as far south as Florida and Texas. Like all snakes, northern water snakes are voracious predators, and they are highly successful due to their broad diets and adaptive characteristics. They're popular prey items for mammals and birds of prey, but their biggest threat is of a two-legged variety: humans.

You may be asking, *Coyote, if they're harmless, why do humans bother them?* Well,

DID YOU KNOW?

Water moccasins live in the southeastern United States and are common in Florida, Alabama, Louisiana, and Texas, although they can live as far north as Kentucky and Missouri.

northern water snakes' banding, coloration, and size are remarkably similar to those of copperheads and water moccasins. These traits, along with their defensive behavior and likelihood to strike, make them seem more sinister than they actually are. If handled by curious humans, these water snakes are notorious for landing at least one painful bite. If that's not enough to deter their capture, they have a few other tricks up their sleeves....

In order to prove their innocence, I decided it was time to feature them in a Brave Wilderness episode and show the Coyote Pack that no matter how many times you're tagged by one of these reptiles, your life is never in danger. Over the course of my life, I have been bitten by the northern water snake more than any other reptile I've encountered and can report firsthand that I have never been seriously injured or affected by their teeth.

Now, I'm sure you're thinking,

YIKES!

Not all nonvenomous snakes are harmless. Boa constrictors and pythons can grow to enormous sizes and can deliver a potentially dangerous bite.

But, Coyote, doesn't that mean they're aggressive?!
It may seem that way, but that's only because I put myself in the line of fire by handling them and provoking a defensive bite in response.

COLUMBUS, OHIO

Ever since I was just eight years old, I've enjoyed catching and admiring these misunderstood reptiles, and since they flourish in my home state of Ohio, I knew just where to look for them. On a cloudy summer morning in June 2018, Mario and I set out to a local nature reserve in Central Ohio to find, catch, and feature this creature for the Coyote Pack. I had been to this location many times and actually caught the largest northern water snake I'd ever seen

at this very spot. Surrounded by cattails and tall grasses, and nestled in a lush forest of shady trees, was our target location: a protected wetland.

Sorry, guys! I can't reveal the exact location of our adventure because it's not accessible to the public, but I have special permits that allow me to explore this wild place. The reason these snakes thrive there is because this natural environment is safeguarded for the species who call this wetland home. In turn, this protection gives valuable insight to researchers about how a balanced ecosystem operates when humans are taken out of the equation.

With that in mind, Mario and I were sure we would spot several northern water snakes, either absorbing the warmth of the summer sun or hunting in the tangled web of pond lilies. To explore a wetland environment like this one, the right equipment is essential. I had my trusty water boots while Mario brought chest-high waders. In our packs we carried our first-aid kit, sunscreen, and lots of water. Good thing, too, because this was about to be a hot and grueling adventure.

When it comes to moving through a mucky, swampy, plant-filled environment, each step comes with its own set of struggles. As we entered the water, I could hear my feet break free from the muck, but just as I was about to step forward, the winding stems of lilies tripped me up.

"Whoa!" I shouted, lunging back with a splash. "I just about fell forward into the water! I guess I'm not used to the terrain yet." I groped around in the reeds in front of me and grabbed on to a sturdy stalk, steadying myself. *GLOP!* This time, I twisted my foot

free from the gooey mess below and trudged through the tangles. Mario, behind me, seemed to be having similar difficulties.

"Dude, it's like quicksand!" He laughed, waddling like a massive penguin as he forced his way forward. From both of us, each leg lift and motion came with a loud splash of water. So far, I hadn't seen a single snake warming itself in the limbs of trees or at the water's edge, but if any were nearby, they probably heard the commotion.

Northern water snakes, like most animals, flee at the first sight of humans. They're hyper aware of their surroundings and, unless they are hidden out of sight, will make a break for the muddy depths of a pond instead of standing their ground. What most people don't realize is that these creatures are more afraid of humans than humans are of them.

We had the whole circumference of the pond to search, and luckily, getting acclimated to the soggy mud didn't take long. With precise steps and watchful eyes, I pored over every tree branch, through every dense patch of plants, and down every embankment, hoping that my gaze would fall upon the slender body of a snake. We plodded through the muck for over an hour but so far hadn't seen a single one.

"It's still overcast," I said, "which is not great for basking snakes." Northern water snakes, like all reptiles, are ectothermic and require warm rays of sun to energize their bodies before they hunt. Whatever the weather, I was still confident we would see them gathering as much energy as they could, and I was determined to catch one before it dove into the pond.

"Oh, what's this?" I said, spotting something on the bank. Reaching down through the thick grasses,

I picked up the pocket-size creature, revealing its hard shell and feet when I opened my hand. "That is a little, tiny painted turtle. He was up on the embankment absorbing some of the sunlight. It definitely didn't expect a predator to come from the water!"

Its shell was just smaller than a soup spoon, and the turtle kept its legs tucked into its shell as I turned it over in my hands. *Not exactly the right kind of meal for a water snake*, I thought, *but there are tons of creatures here who would love a tiny turtle snack!* Cautiously, the turtle poked its wee head out of its shell, probably wondering why it hadn't been eaten yet.

"I'm going to place him back down," I said, admiring the striking red stripes along its skin. "You stay safe out there, little buddy!" Northern water snakes primarily eat fish, frogs, tadpoles, toads, and occasionally small rodents. A turtle's shell—even a baby turtle's—would be a difficult obstacle for a snake to digest.

As we continued our search, bright rays of sun broke through the clouds, renewing my sense of

hope that we'd find our target reptile soaking up the sun.

"This environment is so tough to move through," I said. "The problem is, I'm disturbing the environment a lot, and these snakes can feel vibrations through the water. As I approach, any that could be hiding in the lily pads would dart beneath the surface before I got close.

"Let's keep moving," I insisted. "Since the sun is finally out, I think we still have a good chance of spotting one in the water." It was around noon at this point, so instead of looking on the bank and in the trees, my eyes frantically scanned the spots between each lily pad for signs of scales

or a periscope head poking through the surface. As it turned out, my instincts were correct.

"Mario!" I called. *"SNAKE!"* About twenty yards in front of me, I noticed the round, floppy green pads

move from side to side, and I froze in place. There, peering out of the water, was the dark silhouette of a northern water snake. Mario, who had been searching far behind me, snapped into action. I could hear the splash of his quick steps as he struggled to catch up, but I had to take action.

"I'm making a move on it!" I yelled behind me, slowly moving in for the grab.

"Go for it!" he responded, still rushing to my location.

SNAKE SPOTTED

The snake, sensing the sudden commotion, dipped its head underwater, but I was right on its tail. I lunged forward through the lily pads, my arms outstretched as if I were taking a full dive. *SPLASH!* I was submerged up to my shoulders, but my hands quickly seized the wriggling, slippery body of the snake near its tail. Entangling itself in the vines of the underwater plants, it twisted its body through my fingers, slipping free from my grasp.

"I'm losing it!" I gasped, plunging my arms deeper into the water.

SPLASH!

This time, both hands found their mark, but its strong body was wrapped tightly around the vegetation and I couldn't get it free. The only way to bring it up would be to release one hand, which was close to its head, while the other hand worked it out from the weeds. Losing control over the front end of the snake was a gamble, however, as this would allow the snake to swing around and grab on to my hand with its

Ahh! My finger!

teeth. *I've got no choice*, I thought. *It's worth it not to lose this snake!*

"Ahh!" I hollered, feeling the snake's teeth pierce through my skin. "*Ohh!* It latched on to my finger! *Sst!*" For a few seconds, the snake's puffed-up head squeezed tightly on my pinkie, but I refused to let go. Rearing back, it faced the hand that held it once again, and I could tell it was getting ready for a second strike.

"*Yargh!* Now it's latched on to my arm!" I yelled to Mario, still fighting his way over. "Well, that's what happens when you grab onto the northern water snake—*ouch!*—you stand the chance of taking a pretty good bite!" After about five seconds, the snake let go, its head drooping down in defeat.

WHOA!

The venom of a water moccasin is hemotoxic, and its components lower blood pressure, break down blood cells, and slow down muscle function. It may not be the deadliest of all vipers, but it can still cause massive swelling, infection, and even the loss of a limb!

Normally, I reserve the bite portion of my encounters for the end, but that wouldn't work with this reptile. Nonvenomous snakes like this one typically strike if they've been cornered or caught, attempting to surprise their predator and make their escape. Unfortunately for

this snake, that kind of tactic doesn't faze Coyote Peterson.

"Oh boy, I am definitely bleeding." I smiled. "Took a bite on the finger, and all across my arm. But that's okay! Let's get into a more controlled setting and get this snake up close for the cameras." As though declaring that it wasn't done yet, the snake suddenly lunged toward my face. *Whoa!* Then again, back toward my other arm. *Yikes! I guess you still have some fight in you after all!* I thought, dodging those sharp teeth.

Mario, camera in hand, nestled against the bank of the pond, and I took my place in front of him, the snake still clutched in my fingers.

"Well, that was one arduous search, and in the process, I managed to take a pretty nasty bite." I felt the lingering sting from the snake's teeth on my finger and could see the blood continuing to seep from my skin. The marks on my arm perfectly matched the shape of its jaws, as each puncture was dotted red in a broad oval shape.

"Fear not, guys," I explained. "This is a nonvenomous species, although it is oftentimes mistaken for the venomous water moccasin." At this point, the snake had calmed down. Its head returned to the typical oval shape colubrids are known for, and its body relaxed, no longer puffed up to mimic its venomous cousins.

The northern water snake is a perfect example of animal mimicry. Like vipers with triangular-shaped heads, the northern water snake will suck in air and puff up its head and body, resembling the shape and stout nature of a water moccasin. Some also shake their tails in dry leaves and debris, mimicking the sound of a rattlesnake's famous defensive tactic.

NORTHERN WATER SNAKE

WATER MOCCASIN

"Wow," I said, admiring it up close, "this snake is a pretty good size! Northern water snakes can get up to four feet in length, but this one is about two and a half feet long. Females grow larger than the males, so I'd say that this one is likely a male." I held the

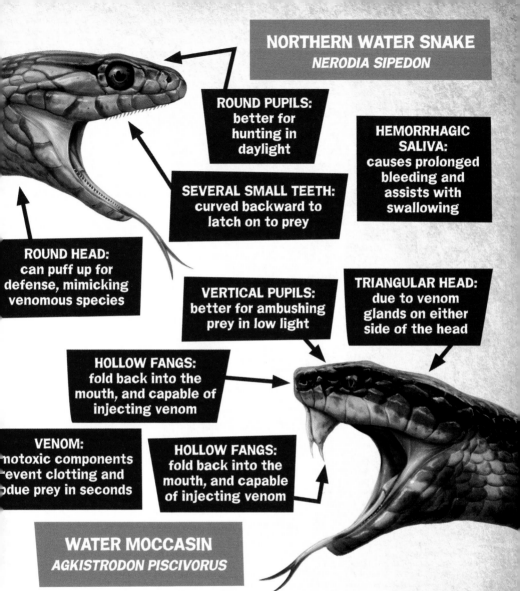

NORTHERN WATER SNAKE
NERODIA SIPEDON

ROUND PUPILS: better for hunting in daylight

HEMORRHAGIC SALIVA: causes prolonged bleeding and assists with swallowing

SEVERAL SMALL TEETH: curved backward to latch on to prey

ROUND HEAD: can puff up for defense, mimicking venomous species

VERTICAL PUPILS: better for ambushing prey in low light

TRIANGULAR HEAD: due to venom glands on either side of the head

HOLLOW FANGS: fold back into the mouth, and capable of injecting venom

VENOM: notoxic components event clotting and due prey in seconds

HOLLOW FANGS: fold back into the mouth, and capable of injecting venom

WATER MOCCASIN
AGKISTRODON PISCIVORUS

snake in one hand, letting him coil up in my palm. Although the snake had mostly calmed down, I could faintly pick up on the last of his defense mechanisms.

"Well, it's not striking at all, but—*sniff sniff*—it is musking, which means it's pooping on me." Almost every snake species uses this tactic, pooping on its predator, to avoid getting eaten. Snake musk is secreted from scent glands near the cloaca and is also

used to mark territory and find mates. Humans could probably do the same thing if confronted by a predator, but we are usually wearing pants.

"Now, if I put my finger just in front of his nose," I said, nearly touching him, "he'll stick out his tongue. Their tongues are able to taste chemicals in the environment, telling the snake if they're likely to be confronted by either predator or prey." Although they have nostrils, snakes smell with their tongues. On the roof of their mouths they have a special sensory organ called a Jacobson's organ, which detects and interprets odor particles brought in by their tongues.

WATER MOCCASIN

NORTHERN WATER SNAKE

"As I mentioned before," I continued, "northern water snakes are often mistaken for water moccasins not only because of their defense mechanism, but also their coloration. One reason I wanted to catch this species is to show you how dark its body is. There is almost no visible banding. When they're younger, that banding is very distinct, but as they get older, it disappears."

It's important to note that of all twenty-five snake species who live in Ohio, only three are venomous: the timber rattlesnake, the massasauga rattlesnake, and the northern copperhead. Many Ohioans have reported seeing the infamous water moccasin in Ohio's waterways, but no biologist has ever documented one, explaining that sightings were most likely a case of mistaken identity.

"I'm just going to dip it into the water for a second," I said, letting him slink through

DID YOU KNOW?

For defense, venomous snakes don't always inject venom, delivering what is called a dry bite. Their venom is primarily used to subdue prey and is a precious resource that takes weeks to produce!

WOW!

Another similarity between the northern water snake and water moccasin is that they both have keeled scales! Each scale overlaps the one after it, and they are perfectly evolved for a snake's streamlined, forward motion.

the surface. "You see how it blends into its environment? In the water you can see how the banding is a little more prominent. That helps to keep them camouflaged between the light and shadows of plant matter."

Venomous water moccasins may not live in Ohio, but northern copperheads do. After seeing the coloration of the northern water snake illuminated by the pond, I could see how some people might mistake its banding for a local copperhead. Copperheads don't often seek water for refuge, however, choosing instead to hide in leaf litter. Their stunning coloration makes them nearly impossible to see, which gives them the perfect cover to ambush approaching prey.

NORTHERN COPPERHEAD

"Well, guys," I said, speaking to the Coyote Pack, "if you go out into a wetland environment and you see one of these snakes, I definitely do not recommend that you try to catch it. While they may not be venomous, their bite is pretty painful. Plus, they have an anticoagulant in their saliva, which will cause you to bleed more than normal."

It had already been about half an hour since the snake bit my arm and finger, and both bite sites were still bleeding. The anticoagulant they produce is actually used to help them subdue and consume their prey. A fish or a frog will quickly go into shock once it's exposed to that chemical, but luckily for me, it has little effect on humans.

"If you are bitten by one, fear not!" I announced. "A little soap and water will clean it right up, and you'll be just fine." If you are ever bitten by a snake and are not able to identify it,

DID YOU KNOW?

In the United States, fatal snake bites are extremely rare. You have a higher chance of being struck by lightning!

I urge you to seek medical attention. Serious injury from snake bites is rare in the United States, but it's always better to be safe than sorry!

"Well, despite the fact that the northern water snake is an incredibly common species, it sure did pose a challenge to find, catch, and get up close for the cameras," I said, giving my final send-off. "I'm Coyote Peterson! Be Brave...Stay Wild—we'll see ya on the next adventure!" And with that, I stepped out into the field of lily pads, thanked my scaly friend, and released him. He may not have been the largest northern water snake I'd ever seen, but he certainly gave me a bite to remember him by.

Once I was out of the water and back on the boardwalk, Mario and I took a little extra time cleaning and bandaging each snake bite to prevent infection. The biggest risk with a bite from any nonvenomous reptile is the bacteria they carry in their mouths or the bacteria from the environment.

The standing pond water I had been in all morning had just as much a chance of causing a problem as the snake's mouth, so I was meticulous in protecting myself from any harmful bacteria.

With my finger and arm bandaged and clean, I packed up my gear. Mario climbed out of his waders, I traded my water shoes for hiking boots, and together we set off down the forested trail, toward the promise of another great adventure.

Over the course of my life, I have been bitten by several varieties of nonvenomous snakes, and I can report firsthand that I have never sustained a serious injury from any of them. Species like the northern water snake, Lake Erie water snake, garter snake, and black rat snake may look threatening, and even resemble some of the deadliest venomous varieties in North America, but the only lasting

impression from their bite is the pain from their numerous sharp teeth, and maybe some mild bleeding.

Every year, people around the globe spot slithering legless reptiles of all shapes and sizes exploring their diverse environments and lying in the glow of the morning sun. Most of the time, these snakes are harmless to humans and they fulfill an essential role in the biodiversity and balance of their ecosystems. Unfortunately for these harmless snakes, they are often linked with their venomous counterparts and strike fear in the minds of any human who may encounter them. From their defensive tactics to their coloration, they employ a number of abilities to deter predators from taking their lives, making them seem far more dangerous than they actually are.

Whenever you're out exploring the natural environment in your hometown, make sure you're aware of your surroundings. A great way to always keep yourself informed is to carry a field guide of your local wildlife, giving you the ability to decide which animals are harmless and which ones to admire from a safe distance. Even if you've explored an environment countless times, you never know what creature may cross your path.

As someone who has had a long-standing fascination and love of these slithering serpents, I've made it my mission to uncover the truth about these reptiles and reveal once and for all that they simply want to be left alone.

CHAPTER 8

THE TERRIBLE AND TERRIFYING TOE BITER!

GIANT WATER BUG

FEAR	✦	✦	✦	✦	✦
IMPACT	✦	✦	✦	✦	✦
DAMAGE	✦	✦	✦	✦	✦
AFTERMATH	✦	✦	✦	✦	✦

TOTAL: 15/20

How do you develop your greatest fear? Is it your imagination creating monsters in the dark? Is it from fairy tales or stories you've heard from those around you? Or is it from a scary, life-changing experience you wish you could forget? Fear comes in many varieties, and believe it or not, we are all—even me—afraid of *something*. For young Coyote, it was the bug in the swamp, and I'm not talking about leeches. I'm talking about a winged, needle-mouthed, water-dwelling insect called the giant water bug, or—as it's commonly known—the toe biter.

I was just eight years old when I discovered my archnemesis. I was out exploring near my home in Newbury, Ohio, on a beautiful, hot summer day.

I was happily wading through the murky pond behind my house when I felt this terrible, piercing pain shoot through my leg. I screamed at the top of my lungs and convulsively wiggled and jumped, trying to get whatever had grabbed on to me *off*.

Panicked, I reached into the dark water, ran my hand under my shorts, and clutched on to a tough, oval-shaped, flat creature bigger than my palm. When I felt its spindly legs flailing in my grasp, shivers shot up my spine, causing my hair to stand on end. I immediately wrenched it from my leg, up and out of the water, and right in front of my face.

I was absolutely horror-struck. A giant, bug-eyed, pincer-armed, beetle-looking grayish-brown insect with a huge beak-like mouth stared back at me. With my leg throbbing in searing pain, I wailed the loudest scream of my life. I shut my bleary eyes, chucked the bug with all my might as far away as possible, and splashed haphazardly through the water and onto the bank.

With one hand clutching my sore leg, I hobbled home yelling for my mom, and crashed into my couch. As she flipped through the pages of a field guide, I pulled aside my shorts to reveal a deep, swollen, bleeding pit that looked like I'd been shot with a staple gun. Tears streamed down my face as my mom asked me what happened.

Unfortunately, she had no idea what I was talking about when I described the insect: *It was b-b-big and b-b-b-brown and had alien eyes and a triangle head and—and it was oval-shaped and had a beak!* Immediately, my mom called the doctor, and for the very first time, I learned the name of my nightmare—the giant water bug.

As it turned out, I would be absolutely fine. Following the doctor's advice, we washed the wound with soapy water and patched it up with a Band-Aid. Then, after about ninety minutes, with an ice pack wrapped around my leg, the sharp pain dissolved into a mild, dull ache that lasted for the rest of the day.

The agony in that first hour was the worst pain I had ever felt in my eight years of life, and I honestly wasn't sure if I would survive. That traumatic

WHOA!

Giant water bugs are the largest true bugs in the world!

experience kept me away from the water for the rest of the year and sealed the horror of the giant water bug in my mind forever. Now, even after confronting the creepiest-crawlies on the planet, I still get the shivers whenever I think of coming face-to-face with my worst nightmare.

Through our travels over the years, Mark, Mario, and I have stumbled across numerous giant water bugs, and every time, the guys would lightly tease me about my childhood fear lasting well into adulthood.

I pretended not to be bothered, keeping my focus on the creatures I was after, but the memory of that terrifyingly painful bite continued to haunt me, and I knew that there was only one way to overcome my fear. If I wanted to conquer this monster once and for all, I would have to revisit that searing pain and take another bite from the terrible toe biter.

By the time I set my sights on this scheme, I had already taken the long-lasting agony of the

DID YOU KNOW?

Lethocerus maximus, a species of toe biter found in South America, is locally called *escorpião d'água,* which is Portuguese for "water scorpion."

bullet ant sting and faced the frightening warrior wasp. As I charged ahead on my journey of *bites*, however, I had begun to discover how vastly different they were from stings. Without question, bites were more painful and tended to have worse consequences.

It was certainly a challenge to confront the fierce creatures I had encountered up to this point, but none so far had provoked the kind of unease and repulsion that the giant water

GROSS!

A giant water bug will let their toxic saliva break down the insides of their prey for up to fifteen minutes before eating it.

bug did. There were very few creepy creatures who gave me nightmares, and next to the giant desert centipede, the toe biter was definitely very high on my list.

In order to make an episode like this happen, my plan was to wait until we came across one naturally. Instead of feeling the anticipation and panic build over weeks before taking the bite, I would have to drum up the courage on the spot. If I was already on location, with gear and cameras at the ready, it would be nearly impossible for me to back down.

COSTA RICA

It took over a year before that fateful encounter would take place, and instead of the familiar swamps of Ohio, we found our foe in the jungle of Costa Rica. I had been to this Central American country several times before, yet had never come across one lurking in the dark waters running through the forest.

Actually, I didn't really know they even lived in Costa Rica, but as our guide and friend Roel de Plecker explained, they were everywhere. Giant water bugs are one of the most common insects in North and Central America. There are twenty-two recognized species in the United States alone, and they are considered the largest "true bugs" in the world.

You may be wondering, *Coyote, aren't all insects bugs?* Actually, only insects with a tubelike proboscis are technically bugs. In other words, "true bugs" suck, while other insects chew. Bugs like bees and butterflies use their proboscises to suck nectar from plants, but some, like the giant water bug, are predatory and suck up the insides of their victims! I know, terrifying, right?!

During one of our nightly jungle excursions, Mark, Mario, and I happened upon one of the largest toe biters I had ever laid eyes on. While scanning the dark ground with my flashlight, I briefly illuminated the camouflaged bug in the shallow swampy water of a small pond. *Rats!* I thought. *Here we go.*

"Guys..." I hesitated. "Guys, guess what I found!" Mark and Mario, flashlights in hand, trotted over to me, expecting to see a venomous snake or sticky frog in my spotlight. "It's a giant water bug!"

Guys, guess what I found!

"I see it!" said Mark, pointing to a nearby log.

"Oh man," said Mario, peering into the water. "You know what that means, right?"

Mark and Mario weren't the only ones who encouraged me to take on the toe biter; the Coyote Pack feverishly called for it, too. After releasing the short clip of one we found in the

Pacific Northwest, it seemed as if every other comment was egging me on to face my fear. Well, guys, I heard you.

"Yeah, yeah. I know what it means." I sighed. "We'll see. First I've got to catch it." Before I could take another step, the giant water bug kicked its powerful back legs and jetted off into the shadows. Carefully, I leaned over the water and spotted it pressed flat against the mud, surrounded by waterlogged leaves.

"It's right on the other side of those plants," I said. "I'm going to go out on that log, and using this net, I'm going to try to scoop it up." I delicately stepped one foot, then the other, out onto the fallen wood, careful not to disturb the environment too much. If I agitated the bottom of the swamp, clouds of thick debris would furl up around the area, making it impossible to see the camouflaged creature I was after.

With both feet steady, I dipped my net silently through the surface and positioned it next to the bug, and then flipped it up, entangling the creature in the mesh. I knew I had it and felt a great sense of both accomplishment and regret.

"*Yes!* Wow, it's big," I said nervously. "Hold on, I'm losing my balance!" The log started to slip under my feet, and with one great leap, I jumped back to solid ground, awkwardly falling to my knees with the toe biter swinging in the net. I urgently turned my attention to the flailing water bug, who was trying desperately to escape its capture. *Oh, no you don't!* I dropped the net, trapping it under the fabric, and took a closer look at my catch.

Wow, it's big!

"That is a monster!" I gasped, uncovering it. With two fingers, I pinched its back, bringing it up to my face. As soon as I picked it up, I felt a lump in my stomach the size of a softball. It was so much bigger than I had realized, and my heart started thumping in my chest.

"Ugh, look at that creature!" I said, steadying my shaking hand. "Like an alien from another planet— that is, the giant water bug—also known as the toe biter." In the eerie darkness of the jungle, soaking wet and exhausted, I came face-to-face with the creature who had haunted me since I was eight years old.

"Huuagh!" I shuddered as the monster flailed its grappling hook arms back at my fingers. "They can fly, they can swim, and their bite is one of the most painful in the insect kingdom." I paused, watching its

ROSTRUM

pointed, beak-like **rostrum** flick up and down as though it were trying to stick me.

"I'm not doing this in the dark, guys," I declared. "But tomorrow morning, I'm going to let my big toe be bitten by the toe biter." With a plastic container in one hand and the lid at the ready, I dropped the beast with a *PLUNK* and fastened the top over it as soon as possible. I could hear the fidgeting of its legs as it scrambled around the bottom, and I quickly stashed it away in my pack.

HOW DO YOU SAY THAT?

Rostrum:
"RAWS-trum"

As I walked back to the lodge, the memory from my childhood ran over and over in my mind, like a scene from a scary movie on repeat. I could remember every sensation and knee-jerking moment, but I had to wonder, *Was it really as bad as I remember?*

Often, the things we experience as children seem bigger, badder, and way scarier than how we might experience them as adults. Was that whole encounter blown out of proportion by my eight-year-old mind? Or would I have the same level of pain and same agonizing reaction as before? I pondered those questions as I lay in bed that night, patiently waiting for sleep to relieve my anxiety.

The next morning, I woke up to the tropical sounds of birds calling through the trees and bolted upright in bed. *Today's the day*, I thought, *that I come toe-to-rostrum with the toe biter.* Surprisingly, I wasn't feeling the same sense of dread that had washed over me the night before. Today I was ready to face my fears and conquer them once and for all.

Near the lodge where we were staying, Mark, Mario, and I prepared our set and got everything into position. On a small table sat the giant water bug, now floating in a cubic container, and once I had my GoPro ready, I took my place in front of the cameras. My sense of

purpose and bravery unshaken, I stared right into the bizarre eyes of the beast before me and started the scene.

"Ever since I was eight years old," I began, "this is the one insect I have truly been afraid of." As I retold the story, I felt the pangs of fear knocking at the back of my head. It was almost as if Coyote from the past were reminding me why I never wanted to see this creature again, but I was determined to overcome my nagging nervousness and pressed on.

"Before we get to the bite," I continued, "let's take a look at this insect's anatomy. There are around sixty species of giant water bug in the world, but they are mostly found in the Americas. The largest size for this species is around four inches, and I'd say this one is pretty close."

GIANT WATER BUG:
LETHOCERUS AMERICANUS

WINGS:
trap air while underwater, also used for flight

RESPIRATORY SIPHON:
allows intake of air while still underwater

ROSTRUM:
mouth part; injects digestive enzymes, sucks up the solution

HIND LEGS:
primarily used for swimming

RAPTORIAL FORELEGS:
modified legs with two hooks that grapple prey

COLORATION:
camouflage adapted to look like fallen debris

Lowering my head down to the bug cube, I estimated that this monster was probably about three and a half inches long. It wasn't difficult to estimate because it floated facedown with its rear toward the surface. Looking closely, I could see a tubelike mechanism extending from its rear, barely breaking the surface, with air bubbles popping out of it when it skittered around at the bottom.

"You see the position that it's in?" I asked. "Look at that snorkel-looking device at the end there. That is actually how it's breathing!"

Mark laughed. "It breathes out of its butt!"

"Right!" I agreed. "It's like a little butt snorkel! That's why they are often seen positioned like that—so they can breathe." Since the toe biter is an aquatic insect, it has several special features adapted to life underwater. Unlike other aquatic creatures, these bugs can't survive underwater without breathing air, and they don't have traditional lungs (like humans) to hold their breath.

Actually, it may surprise you to know that insects don't breathe through their mouths at all! They have spiracles, or openings on their abdomens, that take in air and deliver it to their internal systems. The giant water bug, adapted to life in fresh water, takes it a step further. While under the surface, they use a breathing tube (called a respiratory siphon) to take in and exchange air from a bubble trapped under their wings.

Most female giant water bugs latch on to sunken debris or plants near the surface or float in shallow water, allowing them constant access to the air with their snorkels. When they dive deeper—after food or to avoid predators—the snorkel tucks into their bodies, and they use the air bubble on their backs like a scuba tank until they swim back to the surface! Pretty cool, right?

"What's most intimidating about this creature are those front arms," I said, turning the container toward the camera. "Like all insects, they have six legs, but these front two are modified—those two curved hooks on the end latch on to their food and grapple it into their mouth." For giant water bugs, living life near the surface has its benefits. All sorts of small, semiaquatic creatures have to take a breath now and then, and that's exactly when the toe biter strikes.

"Tadpoles and frogs or fish swimming by are fair game," I continued, "but they can even take down something as large as a duckling. As soon as these insects catch something, they pull it up to their rostrums, which conceal their straw-like

RAPTORIAL FORELEGS

proboscis. The proboscis slides out and injects an incredibly potent saliva into their prey." (Just to warn you, Coyote Pack, this is about to get gross.)

"The toxins in that saliva will actually paralyze their victims while a cocktail of digestive enzymes liquifies their insides. Then, they drink it up—just like a milkshake." *Okay, so maybe I am still scared of the giant water bug,* I thought, after explaining the gory details of a toe biter's table manners. If that doesn't give you the heebie-jeebies, I don't know what will.

Mark, a look of concern on

YIKES!

The saliva of the toe biter is horrifying for humans, but it also numbs their small animal victims, so they don't feel any pain. Still, it's super gross!

his face, asked, "So, is it venom?"

"It's not technically venom," I explained, "but it works like venom." The enzymes and **protease** in the saliva are like acid in your stomach, except they break down the cells in their victims instead of food in their bellies.

"Is that what it's going to do to your toe?" Mark asked, worried.

"I'm not going to let it hold on *that* long," I replied, "but what it is going to do is latch on, and then, *wha-TSCHH*! Whack me with that rostrum. Just a little bit of that saliva is going to be unbelievably painful." A big bug has a big toxic payload, so I knew that its bite would probably be more painful than any of the insect stings I had taken up to this point.

I should explain that the mechanism of injury from a giant water bug may seem like a sting—because of its stinger-like proboscis—but it is technically a bite.

wha-TSCHH!

Although it comes with a dose of toxic saliva, they use their mouth, not their rump, to engage their attack. Think about mosquitoes—they also have a proboscis. That's why when you get those red itchy bumps, you call them mosquito *bites*!

"Ya know," Mark said, "they say that there's a fine line between bravery and stupidity. Where does this fall?"

"This lies in the realm of insanity," I replied. "I still remember the day that I was bitten by one, and it's incredibly painful. You guys are going to see me in unbelievable agony. I've climbed the insect sting pain index, but when it comes to facing my fears of the two creepiest-crawlies in the world, the giant water bug and the giant desert centipede will be on a whole other level."

FUN FACT!

Giant water bugs have excellent camouflage and look just like fallen leaves.

"So, in a way, this will enable you to move past those fears?" Mark asked as I stared blankly at the bug in its container.

"Yeah, a true moment of insane bravery, at least for me."

And with that, I began unlacing the tall snake boot on my left foot, feeling pangs of unease strike my brain with each pull of the shoestrings. I slid out my leg, rolled my sock off my foot, and wiggled my bare toes in the air. I couldn't tell you what Mark and Mario were doing, and I don't even remember setting up my GoPro. All I could think about was the pain I was about to endure, and I could feel the beads of nervous sweat trickling down the back of my neck.

"Ugh!" I grunted, trying to shake the hesitation from my mind. I looked over at the water bug, angrily swimming around its container and thrusting its forelegs at the lid. "This is craziness! I don't know if I can do this!"

"You could just accidentally drop it and let it scurry back off into the water," suggested Mario. *Now there's an idea,* I thought. I looked at my bare foot, back at the toe biter, and up at Mark and Mario.

I don't know if I can do this!

All joking aside, this was a big moment for me. If I didn't go through with it, I knew I'd let not only myself down, but the Coyote Pack as well. I always talk about what it means to be brave, and encourage the audience to overcome their fears, but here I was, thinking about running away from my own.

Now, to be clear, I'm not suggesting that *you* ever intentionally take a bite or sting from something in order to face your fears. For me, however, in order to give my audience insight into what actually happens when bites occur, how it feels, and how to treat it, facing the scary stings and bites of wildlife is part of my job.

I reached up and pressed RECORD on the GoPro and, after seeing the red light, reached for the container. I removed the lid and dipped my fingers into the cloudy water, pinching the toe biter's back on each side, noting how it still

had some eggs hanging on to its body, indicating that my "new friend" was male. He did his best to avoid my grasp and flailed angrily as I lifted him up. I could feel him resisting me with all his strength as he stiffened his back and reached for my hand.

"Whoa! It is so strong!" I remarked, setting the container back on the table. I held the insect a foot from my face, and stared right into his huge black

eyes as I pulled my foot across my lap, just moments away from encountering his daggerlike rostrum.

For a few seconds, I paused, taking deep breaths and shooing away the fearful thoughts that clouded my mind. I could feel my heart begin to race, my hair prickle up and down my arms, and my mouth become dry as a desert. *This is it,* I thought. *My nemesis, my nightmare, it's time to put my fear to rest.*

"Are we ready?" I called out boldly.

"We're ready," Mark quietly replied.

"Okay, here we go," I began, preparing the intro. "I'm Coyote Peterson, and I'm about to be bitten by the toe biter...on my big toe." Not wanting to prolong the inevitable any further, I started the countdown.

On *three*, I moved the giant water bug closer to my foot and felt his sharp forelegs grapple on to my

toe, and instinctively, I shut my eyes. A few seconds dragged past, but all I felt were sharp hooks scratching across my skin. I peeked out of my eyelids, and in that very instant, his head ratcheted down, and his proboscis slid into my flesh like a needle.

Daaarrgh!

"Daaarrgh!" I screamed, feeling searing pain shoot down my foot like a bullet. I immediately let go of the insect, but he held on, pumping more toxic saliva under my skin. In a whirlwind of panic, I pinched him again, removing his rostrum and dropping him to the ground. I could barely focus on what I was supposed to do as adrenaline roared throughout my body.

Recapture him! I said to myself. *Get the container!* Through instinct alone, I haphazardly dumped the container on the ground, scooped up the toe biter, and sealed him in with the lid. Then, feeling the pain intensifying by the millisecond, I stood straight up and jumped on one foot trying to move my digit, which seemed frozen in agonizing pain.

"Aaa-iiieeee-rrrgh!"

I hollered, wildly hopping around the set. My mind was completely blank, overtaken by the burning sensation that was swallowing up my whole foot at this point. I knocked into the table, sending the GoPro tumbling down and me straight to my knees.

It's just as bad a I remembered!

"Gah! Ah! *Ffft!*" I spat, breathing hard through gritted teeth. I clutched my toe, pressing it as hard as I could between my clenched fingers. I had to do something, anything to stop the waves of increasing agony, which was like molten metal oozing through my veins.

"*Oooh-ohh-argh!*" I breathed, barely able to make out the words: "It is just as bad as I remembered!" The unrelenting and unbelievable pain had me on my back, and I screamed at the sky in anguish.

"*Gaaah!* Oh, it's worse," I spat, "than a sting!"

"Dude," Mark said, "you're bleeding!"

I knew I was, but my eyes were shut so tight I didn't even care to see it. All I could

do was feebly attempt to distract myself from what I was feeling, and I rolled over, unable to say anything except, "I hope you guys got the shot!"

Every second felt like minutes, and I had no idea how much time had passed before I finally sprang back to my feet and surveyed the area around me. I couldn't even see the monster in his container, but I could hear him scurrying around, his feet scratching the plastic. I placed my burning foot on the table, huffing and puffing, trying to put words together to describe what I felt.

"Look at my toe," I blurted through pained gasps of air. "The rostrum penetrated deep enough to draw blood, but I was also squeezing it to get out the saliva.

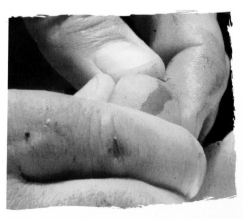

Man, it just screamed in pain immediately!" Losing my balance, I plunged down to one knee, keeping my foot on the table.

"It's really bad," I grunted. "The rostrum is a lot thicker than the stinger of a bullet ant or wasp...." I was getting dizzy and could barely fight my thoughts back into focus from the daze of pain distracting me. My voice was hoarse from screaming, and I was covered in sweat. *Just give the outro*, I thought.

That bite is way worse than any insect sting I've taken.

"The giant water bug has terrified me since I was a little kid," I said. "I spend a lot of time in swamps catching snapping turtles, and every time I jump in, I wonder, *Is this the next time I'll be bitten by the toe biter?* It's just as bad as I remembered." Sweating bullets, exhausted, and nearly out of steam, I finally addressed the audience.

"If you guys come across a giant water bug in the wild, don't try to pick it up. The bite is extremely painful." Running out of breath, I gulped humid air into my lungs. "It is really bad. It's worse than any sting I have ever taken." I closed my eyes, rallied the last of my energy, and delivered my final fleeting thoughts, a message I was reluctant to reveal but that I knew the Coyote Pack would want to hear.

"All right, guys, part one of facing my fears by being bitten by the toe biter has officially happened,"

I said between labored breaths. "Next up, I'm going to be bitten by the giant desert centipede, rumored to have the most painful bite in the creepy-crawler kingdom. I don't know how I'm going to possibly go through that...but stay tuned, guys. I'm Coyote Peterson! Be Brave...Stay Wild—we'll see ya on the next adventure!"

In the end, the agony of the giant water bug's bite only lasted for about ninety minutes. Thirty minutes of searing, intense pain, it took another hour to dissipate, until finally, a dull, uncomfortable ache and persistent itchiness was all that remained.

After filming, I soaked the wound in hot water for several minutes to break down the enzymes of the toe biter's saliva. Then I thoroughly cleaned, disinfected, and dried my big toe before placing some Neosporin and a Band-Aid across the top. It was still sensitive and uncomfortable, but I could walk just fine once the initial pain subsided.

If *you* are ever bitten by one of these insects, however, listen to your body. Everyone experiences things differently, and it's always best practice to seek medical attention if you or your parents or guardians feel you're in danger.

———

Facing my fear of the giant water bug took more courage than any of the stings I've intentionally taken before. I'm sure you're wondering whether I'm still scared of them or not, and the answer is: of course! But not in the same way.

By taking the bite of the giant water bug, I realized that sometimes we are afraid of things for a reason. When I say *Be Brave*, I'm talking about bravely exploring the natural world, appreciating all the amazing creatures who share it with us, and admiring them instead of handling or harming them. When I say *Stay Wild*, I mean leave these animals and critters where they belong, in the natural world they call home.

When I encourage you, the Coyote Pack, to face your fears, I mean don't be afraid of things that can hurt you...but give them the space and respect they deserve. Each of these amazing creatures has adapted potentially harmful abilities in order to survive. So, if you come across a giant water bug on your adventures, don't worry!

These bugs aren't like homing missiles, going after every human who enters their watery environments. They, like all creepy-crawlies, just want to be left alone. If you don't bother them, they won't bother you. If you ever see one, take my word for it: Picking it up is not worth the pain of its bite. Just admire this creature from a safe distance and keep yourself out of harm's way.

CHAPTER 9

A MONSTROUS MISTAKE!

GILA MONSTER

SAVAGE SCALE

FEAR

IMPACT

DAMAGE

AFTERMATH

TOTAL:

17 / 20

If I were a kid and had something as cool as YouTube at my disposal, what animals would I want to learn about? What animals would my friends want to learn about? Those are the questions that drove me and the Brave Wilderness crew across the globe, seeking out incredible creatures and adventures. Soon, however, questions directly from our audience were what motivated us, and since this book is all about the bites I've taken, I'm sure you know what questions I'm talking about!

The first *extreme* video we ever produced on the channel happened in the early days of Brave Wilderness, when I was intentionally quilled by a porcupine. From there, the demand to see me perform dangerous stunts became a rather common request and the Coyote Pack couldn't wait to see what was next.

Time after time, I delivered. After thorough preparation and important advice from animal experts, I've intentionally taken on some of the scariest, most pain-inducing creatures on the planet. The key word there is *intentionally*. Days of research and planning, plus a crew of trained professionals, are what allow me to perform these outrageous stunts, and because of that, we always know exactly what to do if something goes wrong. But what about when things happen *by accident*?

That's exactly what this chapter is all about! Sometimes, all the knowledge, experience, and preparation are not enough when you're confronted with something unexpected. And let's be honest: Everyone makes mistakes. In 2015, I learned a hard lesson from one such mistake when I took the worst, most painful accidental bite of my life. Allow me to introduce you to the United States' only venomous lizard,

THE GILA MONSTER

Gila monsters are uncommon to see, even for the most well-traveled and experienced reptile enthusiasts. They're well-known for their hard, beaded scales; bright aposematic coloration; thick, robust tails; razor-sharp teeth; and venomous bites. Shrouded in mystery and seldom seen, these cryptic creatures can be found only in the deserts, rocky foothills, and dense scrublands of the southwestern United States.

WOW!

Surprisingly, Gila monsters can live at elevations of up to five thousand feet!

Gila monsters don't roam vast stretches of desert, preferring to spend most of their lives close to home. They only venture off for the promise of food or mates and can sometimes be seen duking it out with

trespassing rivals in fierce territorial battles. With short, stocky limbs, they aren't the fastest lizards on the planet, and their lumbering gait makes catching prey a challenge.

Instead of chasing after food, however, Gila monsters sniff it out. With their long forked tongues, they sense the air around them, following a chemical trail until they find their feast. It's not swift-footed mice they're after, or even land-dwelling birds like quail. Instead, they seek the scent of ground birds' nests or the burrows of small mammals and other lizards.

Upon finding their prize, they dine on whatever might be inside, including eggs, hatchlings, or even baby mammals. When one of these beasts eats, they don't stop until the food is completely gone. In a single meal, they can consume about a third of their total body weight. For a ten-year-old human, that would be like eating the whole turkey (plus stuffing) at Thanksgiving dinner! When you live in the desert, however, you never know when you'll find your next meal, and a large feast can sustain an adult Gila monster for weeks.

So, why am I telling you all about Gila monsters? Well, keep reading, and I'm sure you'll find out!

SONORAN DESERT

In 2015, the Brave Wilderness team and I were once again filming in Tucson, Arizona, home of the Sonoran Desert. This beautiful mountainous landscape is one of our favorite places to explore because of its iconic plant life, rich ecosystems, and incredible biodiversity. With over three hundred native birds, sixty native mammals, thousands of arthropods, and over one hundred native reptiles, the Sonoran Desert is actually the most diverse desert in North America! It's no wonder we keep coming back!

The best time of year to search for creatures in this location is late August and early September, when the

WHAT'S IN THE NAME?

The Gila's scientific name *Heloderma* means "studded skin."

monsoon rains quench the parched earth. As the water brings grasses and dried plants back to life, the animals and insects who depend on these resources for survival burst onto the scene, making a mad grab for as much of the bounty as possible.

Since prey items are active, so, too, are predators, and that is exactly what Mark, Mario, and I were counting on. That year, our big goals were fast-footed lizards, interesting arachnids, and one of the most venomous rattlesnakes in the world, the Mojave.

In the early days of the trip, we roamed the washes and foothills of private ranch land, scouring every burrow, bush, and basking spot. Our search for diurnal species started early each morning and

lasted until the heat of the sun banished us back to the safety of the air-conditioning. When the sun finally began to set, we'd gear up again and make our way back to the desert wilderness, hunting for nocturnal creatures in the cooler nighttime temperatures.

On one such morning, after several successful days of filming, we set out to snag a few extra shots of the environment to include in our episodes. Before sunrise, the three of us packed into our vehicle, drove thirty minutes farther into the wilderness, and started winding our way through the washes as the sun's warm glow peeked over the mountains.

We weren't actually searching for animals at that point, as we had already found a ton of and filmed several great species in the days beforehand. In my experience, however, encounters with incredible creatures often happen when you least expect them.

Looking for picturesque patches of desert, I trudged through the thick brush, dodging cactus thorns and mounds of stinging ants. My eyes darted from hazard to hazard, when, all of a sudden, I caught a glimpse of something orange and black, partially hidden by a dried-up piece of wood. I took a few steps back, peered around the debris, and then called out to my companions.

"Mario! Mark!" I hollered behind me. "Check it out!" Mario, just few yards away, ducked around bushes and spiny branches until he was standing next to me. I pointed down to the ground and said...

"Can you believe it?...A Gila monster!"

As I mentioned before, seeing one of these stunning lizards is incredibly rare. About 90 percent of the Gila monster's life is spent underground in burrows, so even if they're close by, your chances of spotting one are slim. Some reptile enthusiasts will go their entire lives searching and never even catch a glimpse, so we knew this was a special moment.

"Guys, what is it?" Mark asked, catching up

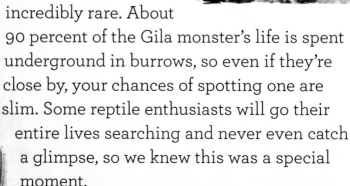

to us. Mario and I pointed to the large lizard before us, barely able to make out the words: "Gila monster!"

"Oh, cool," Mark said, "but we already got a Gila monster episode last year, guys."

"I know, I know, but can you believe it?" I beamed, absolutely stunned by our luck. "It's a big one, too! We've got to get some shots of it."

Mario, an avid photographer, already had his camera in hand and was crouched low, snapping shot after shot. Instantly, I grabbed my GoPro, ready to follow suit.

It's important to mention at this point that throughout all this human activity, the Gila monster barely moved at all. Content to absorb the first rays of morning sun, and not seeing us as a threat, it calmly tolerated the excited observers around it. It lazily flicked out its black tongue, sensing the air, and always kept a watchful eye on us, prepared to strike if we got too close.

Normally, if a Gila monster feels threatened, it makes a show of warning to you. First, it will slowly turn its body to face you, letting out a series of low, subtle

DID YOU KNOW?

Gila monsters may be voracious predators, but they only need to eat about once a month. That's because they store extra fat from big meals in their tails!

HISSSSSSSS

hisses. Then it will raise its blocklike head, open its mouth to reveal the dark-purple interior, and let out a long defensive hiss, saying, *I'm telling you to back off!* If that doesn't work, the agitated lizard snaps into action, whipping its body around in a flash and striking aggressively with open jaws at its pursuer.

When faced with predators, like hawks or coyotes (the animal kind, not me), this impressive creature has one more built-in defense. From head to tail, Gila monsters are protected by beadlike bony deposits covered in scales—called osteoderms. This

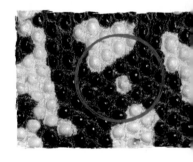

specialized armor keeps the lizard guarded from teeth and claws, giving it the opportunity to defend itself or escape into the nearest burrow.

Much to my delight, this particular monster was as cool and collected as they come, and neither Mario nor I heard a single hiss. Eagerly, I got closer to the ground, marveling at its beautiful peach-

Don't get any closer!

and-pale-orange coloration. *What a robust lizard*, I thought. *It's the biggest I've ever seen!* End to end, it was over a foot and a half long, and it had a thick hefty tail and beady black eyes.

"Coyote," called Mark, his camera focused on my approach. "What's going on right now?"

"Well, guys," I began, "this is the second Gila monster that we've encountered in the Sonoran Desert. He doesn't want anything to do with us, and is just lying low in the sand saying, *Okay, don't get any closer.*"

FUN FACT!

Gila monsters are closely related to beaded lizards, which are also painfully venomous lizards living in the deserts of Mexico.

I should have followed my own advice.

For about five minutes, I knelt on the pebbled ground and, inch by inch, got my camera daringly close to the Gila monster's feet, scales, tail, and head. I was so absorbed in what I was seeing on the screen of my GoPro that I let my mind ignore all my knowledge, training, and experience in order to get what I thought was the footage of a lifetime.

———

At this point in my career as a wildlife expert, I had worked with many varieties of venomous creatures, including Gila monsters. Under all previous circumstances, I'd always had my guard up, especially when working with potentially deadly pit vipers like rattlesnakes.

Rattlesnakes in particular can move at incredible speeds and, when they strike out, can launch themselves up to half their body length in any direction! With fangs like full syringes, they forcefully inject their victims with venom, then slither off to make a hasty escape. Pit vipers like rattlesnakes utilize these strengths for both hunting and defense.

Gila monsters, on the other hand, are an entirely different story. From my experience, the striking distance of a full-size adult is no more than six inches, and although they whip around in the blink of an eye, they're not able to reach much farther in front or behind them without slowly walking there first.

As for the bite, it's hard to estimate the venom yield of a Gila monster, because their mechanisms for introducing venom are very different from the hinged fangs of pit vipers. Instead of two hollow hypodermic needles, these lizards' bottom jaws can have up to eighteen long, fixed, lance-shaped teeth, fitted with grooves. Their venom is produced in the glands under their jawbone, and when they bite, it works its way into their saliva, then flows up the channel-like grooves in their teeth, slowly seeping into their victims.

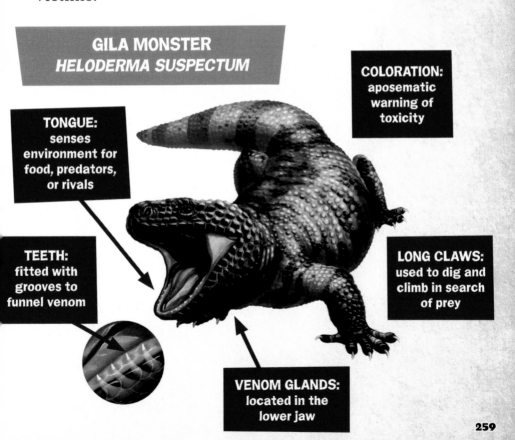

GILA MONSTER
HELODERMA SUSPECTUM

COLORATION: aposematic warning of toxicity

TONGUE: senses environment for food, predators, or rivals

TEETH: fitted with grooves to funnel venom

LONG CLAWS: used to dig and climb in search of prey

VENOM GLANDS: located in the lower jaw

Unlike rattlesnakes, they don't often need to use venom when subduing prey, so its primary use is defense. Once they've made contact, Gila monsters tighten their bite and refuse to let go, constantly working their jaws to introduce as much venom as possible. Although their venom is potent, it's rarely life-threatening to humans. Instead, the neurotoxins of Gila venom induce an unimaginable pain that builds over time, a sensation I wouldn't wish on my worst enemy.

So, there I was, inching my way closer and closer to the Gila monster in front of my GoPro, laser-focused on the screen in my hands. Now, you may be wondering, *Coyote, shouldn't you be focused on the animal?!* As I was about to learn, yes.

I remember thinking, *I can't believe how close it's letting me get!* Then, all of a sudden, as I greedily repositioned myself to get one last sweeping shot over the length of its body...the monster snapped into action.

In a flash, it spun its body around with a jolt of power and, with its mouth wide open, latched on to the edge of my thumb! The force from its movement knocked the GoPro clean out of my hands, and in a moment of pure instinct, I ripped my thumb out of its razor-sharp teeth, tearing several cuts through my skin.

"*Aaaaahhhhrrrrrgh!*" I screamed, leaping backward. "Brugh!" I flung my hand in the air,

No, no, no!

my eyes darted to the injury. My head swarmed with disbelief as I pored over the ten slices in my skin, now oozing with blood. Immediately, searing pain roared up my thumb like wildfire, and I knew this was a

It's burning really bad!

very bad bite. *What was I thinking?! What a dingus!*

"What happened?" Mark called.

"He got me!" I yelled, feeling a heavy sense of panic crash down on my body. *No, no, no!* My mind was racing, trying to deny the critical mistake I had just committed.

Mark rushed over, camera in hand, with Mario close behind him. Bent over, feeling as if I might puke, I squeezed my injured hand with all my might, desperately trying to keep the venom from spreading.

"He got you?" Mark asked skeptically. "You don't mean..."

"Yeah, he got me," I grunted. "He definitely bit me." Mark still looked confused, not fully able to comprehend how I could have let myself get bitten by the slowest venomous reptile in the desert.

"Oh my gosh, it burns already," I blurted out in a rush. "It's burning really bad!"

"Let's go," Mario demanded, leaping into action. "I'll get the gear."

"How?" Mark asked. "How did it happen?" Utterly shocked and not sure what to do, he continued to film.

"Huuurgh!" I growled through clenched teeth.

"He went past the GoPro and got the whole top of my thumb." As though the searing pain weren't strong enough to begin with, it continued to build with every throbbing pulse of my heart. My mind was going blank, unable to focus on anything but the mounting agony I was faced with. I sucked in the dry air as a combination of embarrassment and fear swarmed my mind.

"Just stop," I spat. "Stop filming."

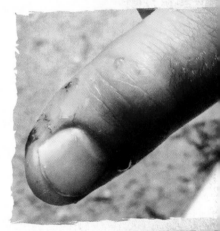

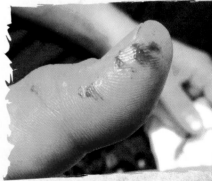

Mario brought us all our backpacks, filled haphazardly with the equipment we'd brought, and we hastily started the thirty-minute walk to our car. With every staggered step, I could feel the building, burning, sharp pain spread just a little bit

OUCH!

Unless they're eating eggs that are too big for their mouths, Gila monsters swallow them whole! What a monstrous meal!

farther. I would have lost my marbles if it weren't for my friends, constantly coaching me to remain calm.

"Coyote," Mario said as we flung open our car doors, "I have one bar of cell phone service. Do you need an ambulance?" I looked up at him through bleary eyes and wiped the sweat from my face, shaking my head.

I know what you're thinking, *What?! Coyote, this is an emergency!* The pain was overpowering, sure...but remember, Mario and I are wildlife experts, and from our experience and knowledge, we knew I wasn't in immediate danger. After careful consideration, I recalled that my thumb had met the Gila monster's teeth for only one second before I pulled it back, and I convinced myself that there couldn't have been much venom in that swift exposure.

Plus, we were in the middle of nowhere! An ambulance would probably have taken an hour to arrive, and since there is no antivenom for gilatoxin, a hospital would do little more than manage my pain. I thought hard about my situation, and even though I was in more agony than ever, I wasn't having an abnormal reaction to the Gila monster venom.

If I were having trouble breathing or had lost consciousness, trust me, Mario would have called 911 as soon as we had service. Any venomous animal has the potential to incite an allergic reaction, and no matter how nonthreatening *you* think the venom is, you should always seek medical attention and leave treating a venomous bite to professionals.

In this situation, we carefully monitored my symptoms, all of us on high alert for any change in my condition during the bumpy drive back. The whole way,

Mario talked me through the pain, kept me calm, and kept a watchful eye on the swelling wounds, which continued to bleed profusely.

WOW!

Gila monsters' tough armored scales cover every part of their bodies except their bellies!

Twenty minutes later, we were back at base camp. I burst through the door and feverishly opened the faucet, running my hand under the cool water to clean out the wound and get any residual venom off my finger. By now, the burning sensation had oozed past my wrist and felt like slow-moving molten lava, unfurling a white-hot, blinding pain on every nerve, muscle, and blood vessel it touched. I could barely feel the water, and if anything, it seemed to make the pain worse.

While Mark bandaged my swollen thumb, Mario got on the phone, calling every reptile expert he could think of to find out more about Gila monster venom. I can imagine their disbelief at hearing what had happened, but unfortunately for me, they all had the same advice.

"Sorry, Coyote, I tried," Mario said, defeated. "There's nothing that can stop it. It's going to keep getting worse until it gets better. We just have to keep you as calm as possible and continue to monitor your symptoms. You're going to have to tough it out."

I can't really remember much from those agonizing hours other than the pain. From the time I realized what had happened, it was as if my mind were suspended in deep space, focused on nothing but the neurotoxin ravaging my body. I think it had been three hours when the pain reached my elbow, and I remember feeling like someone had poured boiling plastic over my bones, stiffening them until I couldn't move my arm.

For lunch, I ate Popsicles, and as much as I prayed for sleep to carry my mind away, I couldn't sit still. My body squirmed in discomfort as I tried to watch my favorite movies, but nothing could pull my mind away from my predicament. I tried walking outside, thinking that fresh air might help, but after just a few minutes, a dizziness overtook my balance and I headed back to the couch. It's hard to describe how intense the pain was at this point, and just as Mario had said, it only continued to get worse.

After four more excruciating hours, it took every ounce of restraint I had not

DID YOU KNOW?

Gila monsters can climb! The sharp claws on their feet help them grapple onto rocks, trees, and cacti. Typically, you won't find them high above ground, as they only do this to flee from predators or find a clutch of eggs.

to scream when the lavalike sensation oozed up to my shoulder. Once it got to the top of my arm, it felt like hot embers exploding in bursts. Then I felt a tight searing pressure, like a fiery phantom

reaching through my skin, squeezing my joint in its grasp. I jumped up in pain, paced around the small room, and breathed hard, now worried about what would happen when it reached my chest.

The fear and anxiety of venom reaching my vital organs consumed me, and instead of trying to be tough, I was ready to get professional help. Then, just as I was about to surrender and head for the hospital, it started to dissolve. With pins and needles, the furious feeling receded, allowing me to breathe a sigh of relief that my nightmare might finally be over.

Altogether, the intensity of the venom lasted for about eight hours before slowly dissolving over the course of the evening. I'm extremely fortunate that throughout the entire day, Mark and Mario remained steadfastly by my side, continuing to check on me and give me encouragement. *You can tough through this, Coyote. You're strong. Coyote, drink some water. Coyote, we're here for you.*

The next morning, I woke up feeling like the luckiest guy alive. My thumb was still swollen and sore, but other than some lingering tenderness, my hand would be absolutely fine. The several small cuts were a deep purple, but all of them healed within a few weeks. If I had been bitten by any one of the United States' venomous snakes, I would likely have lost my thumb to cell-destroying cytotoxins or a lasting infection.

Normally, bite and sting episodes are well-thought-out demonstrations that hopefully educate our viewers about the animals, the effects, and the aftermath of the encounter. It's one thing to read about a bite or sting, but it's another to actually see it happen. Watching the teeth of an alligator make contact with my skin or seeing the stinger of a bullet ant as it buries deep into my arm gives viewers a much different perspective than hearing someone recount the experience would.

In every bite and sting episode, I painfully describe the sensations I'm feeling and show the Coyote Pack what happens as a result. So, when I'm asked, *Why do you do it?*, it's because if I were a kid, seeing it all firsthand would give me a much better understanding and education than just reading bite symptoms on a chart.

When I take bites and stings on camera, I am always very careful and very prepared, and know how to keep myself and my crew safe. Normally, I never put myself in situations that could cause me permanent harm, which is why I would never *intentionally* take a bite from a Gila monster or any venomous reptile in the United States. It simply isn't worth the risk.

After having made such a horrible venomous blunder, however, I've learned a valuable lesson. No matter how docile they seem, no matter how calm, a wild animal will always defend itself. I knew better than to get that close. I had seen Gila monsters thrash defensively before and knew how fast they strike. The Gila monster didn't seem stressed or threatened, but just one wrong move triggered a defensive response, and I was too close to avoid it. Lured into a false sense of security, I severely underestimated that marvelous lizard, and it was ultimately my fault that I was bitten.

As the saying goes, *Only a fool gets bitten by a Gila monster.* I can truly say that was one of the most foolish moments of my entire career, but my Gila monster bite now serves as a lasting lesson that even wildlife experts like me make mistakes.

I hope that through my misstep, I have shown *you,* the Coyote Pack, how important this lasting message is: Never interact with dangerous animals. Safety isn't just about carrying a first aid kit and drinking water. No matter what habitat you're exploring, always be aware of your surroundings with keen eyes and sharp ears so that, when one of the planet's majestic creatures does cross your path, you can have the right kind of encounter. You are a guest in nature, visiting the home of wild animals who live there, and as Coyote Peterson learned the hard way, it's always best to admire these creatures from a safe distance.

CHAPTER 10

DO CENTIPEDE MAKE COYOTE CRY?!

GIANT DESERT CENTIPEDE

SAVAGE SCALE

FEAR

IMPACT

DAMAGE

AFTERMATH

TOTAL: 20/20

If you've ever turned over a log in the woods, you're probably familiar with the variety of crawling, skittering insects and critters who live underneath. You might see beetles, with their shiny black exoskeletons, or maybe ants, sprawling in all directions to escape. You could find harmless, curled-up millipedes, guarding themselves from danger. But watch out! One of these multi-legged creatures, and the creepiest of them all, might find you first.

You've seen them under flowerpots, with short, stout legs and red heads. Maybe you've even seen them in

DID YOU KNOW?

Arthropods classify anything that has an exoskeleton instead of a bony skeleton, including crustaceans!

your house, with long spindly legs and wormlike bodies. If you know what I'm talking about, you know how fast they dart around, and you've probably felt their chilling appearance send shivers up your spine. That's right, I'm talking about centipedes.

HOW DO YOU SAY THAT?

Myriapod:
"MIR-ee-uh-pod"

Centipedes are not technically insects. Although they are related, centipedes and millipedes are classified as **myriapods**. As you know, insects have three body segments—a head, thorax, and abdomen—whereas myriapods always have anywhere from eight to over a hundred, and each segment has at least one pair of legs. Myriapods live all over the world but thrive in tropical climates. They come in all shapes and sizes and are generally classified in one of two categories: centipedes or millipedes.

Now, even though they look creepy, millipedes are relatively harmless to humans. Even the largest species doesn't bite, but they do have a unique defense mechanism that releases a toxin

YIKES!

Some species of millipedes have a unique defense mechanism that releases a toxic substance—hydrochloric acid—from their bodies, giving whatever is handling them a nasty burn.

from their bodies that can be irritating to the skin and dangerous if swallowed. Other than that, they are relatively safe to interact with. Centipedes, however, can and *will* bite humans....

That doesn't mean that they're out to get you! Like all creatures, they just want to be left alone. If threatened, however, they can deliver a nasty bite with their modified front legs, which is accompanied by long-lasting pain and swelling. Did you know that most centipedes are venomous?

Most of the time, these small creatures are relatively harmless, preferring to chow down on dead plant material, insects, or spiders. Small varieties, like the house centipede, can still bite, but it's no more painful than a bee sting. Larger species, however, like the giant desert centipede, can deliver some of the most painful, long-lasting, terrible bites of the creepy-crawler kingdom.

As I shared in Chapter 8, the only two creatures who truly give me nightmares are the giant water bug and the giant desert centipede. Both are absolutely terrifying creatures with extremely painful bites, not to mention their chilling oversize appearance and monstrous mouths.

As a kid growing up in Ohio, I had encountered the giant water bug before, but the only centipedes I had seen were the small ones scurrying around in my backyard. I knew they could bite and I'd heard the bite was painful, but I wasn't particularly afraid of them.

WHOA!

About three thousand species of centipedes have been identified worldwide!

I'd seen plenty of stinging insects and venomous arachnids before, so why be afraid of centipedes?

Well, one summer my family went to Arizona on vacation, and I came face-to-face with the ultimate myriapod monster. As I casually flipped over a flat piece of wood in the desert, one of these shifty beasts darted straight at me! I yelled, dropping the wood and jumping back, absolutely terrified as it scurried through the sand toward my feet. It was half a foot long, had about forty-two pointy legs, and was plated with orange-yellow-and-black armor all the way down its flexible body. *YURGH!* It gives me the creeps just thinking about it.

At that time, I hadn't been bitten by this monster and didn't even know that they were venomous, but it made no difference. Its appearance alone was enough to keep these creatures crawling into my nightmares, and that is where they have stayed throughout my life.

Giant desert centipedes are only one of the many supersize varieties who live across the globe. In the Sonoran Desert, however, they are known as a true menace and have had a few run-ins with locals that I was horrified to hear about.

One of these encounters happened to a friend of mine and fellow wildlife expert Phil Rakoci, better known as Wildman Phil. One day, he was doing a demonstration at a local arboretum with one of these myriapods and was accidentally bitten. At first, he wasn't in horrible pain, but over the course of several hours, he said that it was so excruciating, he had to go to the hospital.

I want to point out that Wildman Phil is one of the toughest guys I know. Over his career, he has taken multiple accidental bites and stings from truly scary things like rattlesnakes and tarantula hawks. When Phil says that the giant desert centipede's bite is worse than a rattlesnake's bite, he

means it, and I trusted his advice when he told me, *It's a bite you never want to experience.*

In 2017, after climbing my way up the insect sting pain index and taking bites from multiple monstrous creatures, I was ready.

For the Coyote Pack, ending on the giant desert centipede's bite would be a truly fitting finale, as you repeatedly asked me, *Coyote, when are you going to face the giant desert centipede?!* But I wasn't sure I would be willing to take it on.

Mark and Mario were on the fence

about it, too, especially after watching me go through the volcano-like aftermath of the accidental Gila monster bite.

I'd filmed with giant desert centipedes several times over the years and each time felt the same knee-jerking, squeamish reaction from their freaky, fidgety bodies. Knowing from Phil how intensely painful their bite was, I considered that maybe this creature's bite would be *too* painful and *too* extreme. *Is it worth the risk? Will this creature be the last stop on my path of intentional bites?* Unable to draw a conclusion for myself, I decided to let fate decide.

SONORAN DESERT

In the fall of 2017, we embarked upon one of our last trips of the year, and there's no better place to find a multitude of amazing creatures to feature on the Brave Wilderness channel than Arizona. If I happened to stumble upon the giant desert centipede, I'd make my final decision at that moment.

Over several nights, we trekked through the rocky desert terrain looking for cryptic creatures looming in the shadows. The thought of meeting a giant myriapod was always in the back of my mind, but at this point, it wasn't my goal to find one. I knew these centipedes were primarily nocturnal, and we had seen them on every trip to the Sonoran Desert. So, it came as no surprise when on our final night of filming, we spotted the biggest centipede I'd ever seen.

"Centipede!" I yelled, my flashlight bouncing over the ground. "It's right under this bush." Mark and Mario rushed forward, cameras recording every moment as I tried to grasp the centipede's flat body with snake tongs.

"Oh no," I murmured. "It's moving. Give me the plastic container!" The multi-legged critter wouldn't be caught so easily and darted around the desert alarmingly fast.

"Use your hat!" Mark suggested. Without a second thought, I dropped it over the creature, but again, it evaded the trap.

"It's not working," I exclaimed, trying to corner it. "I can't grab on to it! Maybe if I get it pinned..." Gently, I pushed the edge of my

cowboy hat onto the centipede's armor-plated back just as Mario sprinted over with the container. Wriggling free, the centipede reared up at its pursuers, but just as it was about to retreat into the shadows, I scooped it up in the plastic box.

"Whoa!" We all gasped. "Got it!" Frantically, I closed the lid, running my hands along the edges to triple-check that it couldn't escape.

"That will get your heart racing," I said, a bit frazzled. "The bite from this creature is one of the most painful in the Southwest, and if there is one creature that intimidates me, it is the giant desert centipede. *Wow!* That is a big one!" I held my flashlight up to the enclosure, illuminating its dozens of bright-yellow legs.

"That is creepy, man," Mark said, looking repulsed.

"Yeah, it's a living nightmare!" I replied. "I can't tell you how many people have requested that I get bitten by this thing." I felt the centipede's hooked legs scratching the plastic through the container and shuddered. *Why did I have to find the biggest one?* I wondered. *Am I really going through with this?*

"I can see your gears grinding," Mark added. "It's got me a little nervous."

"Well, I'm definitely not going to do it under the darkness of night," I replied. "What I might be willing to do is sleep on it and

This centipede is the largest I've ever seen and is maximum size for the species at eight inches long!

consider it again tomorrow under daylight. Right now, I'm thinking no way, most of me is incredibly fearful, but...part of me is curious."

"I don't know if I'm comfortable with that, Coyote,"

Mark said hesitantly. "This might be a bite too far." I could understand his reluctance, but ultimately, the decision was up to me. *If* I took the bite of the giant desert centipede— and that was a big *if*—it would be the best way to end my run of voluntary painful encounters on YouTube for good.

As we made our way back to base camp, I carefully considered my options. In the end, it came down to this: *What am I willing to go through to show the Coyote Pack the effects of the centipede's bite?*

I woke up the next morning just as the sun broke over the dark mountains. Picking up the plastic container, I examined the angry-looking creature we had captured the night before. Taking in a long and slow breath, I harnessed my inner bravery and knew I could face this fear. My mind was made up—I was going to take a bite.

Before the scorching heat of the afternoon set in, we prepped our scene. The temperature was hovering

at a comfortable eighty degrees. That was pleasant compared to the one-hundred-degree heat that was certain to arrive around midday. Overnight, the

centipede had stayed nestled in a cool, dark enclosure, but it was time to transfer it into a clear bug cube. Goose bumps raised on my arms as I delicately tipped the leggy beast out of its temporary container into its main-stage

presentation cube.

As soon as we were set up, Mark and Mario raised their cameras and hit RECORD, and I walked into the sunlit scene.

"When they say *giant desert centipede*, they aren't kidding," I noted. "Look at the size of that myriapod. Wow, it's even more intimidating in the daylight than it was last night.

"It's now seven o'clock in the morning, and I think we all know what's going to happen.... I'm gonna do it. I'm going to take the bite so that I can fully explain to you how painful it really is." That was that. Fully committed, I looked up at the faces of my friends. They both looked concerned but gave me a firm nod, saying, *All right, Coyote, we're with you.*

"Before we get into the bite," I continued, "let's take a look at the anatomy of this creature. It's the perfect design for everything that is creepy.

"This centipede is the largest species in the United Sattes, and they are primarily nocturnal," I said, glancing down at the furious, squirming centipede. It was frantically trying to run up the sides of

FUN FACT!

The Amazonian giant centipede is the longest in the world, reaching lengths of up to twelve inches! That's a foot-long nightmare!

the plastic cube in an attempt to either escape or attack. Honestly, it was tough to tell at this point.

"Ever since I was a little kid," I said, "I've thought, *Yikes, I don't want to get near that thing!* because they have so many legs and each one has a little hook on it. When they grab onto something, they *really* hold on. And when they bite, those fangs ratchet down and don't let go. Ugh, I can hear its little legs scratching on the inside of this capsule." Have you ever heard nails on a chalkboard? *Scree-scree-scree-scree-scree!*

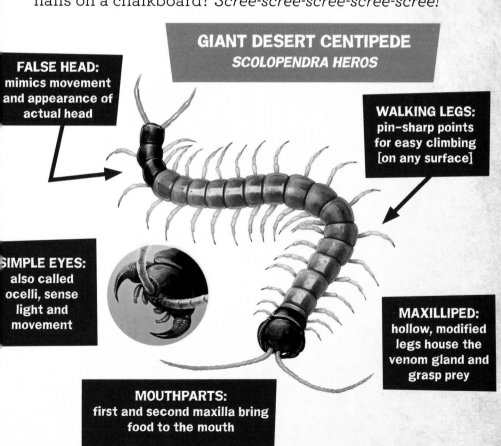

GIANT DESERT CENTIPEDE
SCOLOPENDRA HEROS

FALSE HEAD: mimics movement and appearance of actual head

WALKING LEGS: pin–sharp points for easy climbing [on any surface]

SIMPLE EYES: also called ocelli, sense light and movement

MAXILLIPED: hollow, modified legs house the venom gland and grasp prey

MOUTHPARTS: first and second maxilla bring food to the mouth

Now, I call it a centipede *bite*, but technically it's like a combination of a sting, pinch, and bite all in one. Giant desert centipedes have modified legs in front of their mouths called maxillipeds. They are like stingers in that they inject venom, and are like pincers because they grasp prey like claws do. Because they are located on the head and are grasping mechanisms for the mouth, I classify the venom-injecting, pain-inducing pinching grasp of these modified legs as a bite.

"When I've been stung by things in the past, I hold on to them with the entomology forceps, and when I let go of the insect, it usually falls right off my arm. In this instance, the animal is capable of holding on to me and inflicting more than one bite.

"I know you guys want to get a better look at this

HOW TO TELL THE DIFFERENCE!

The similar head and tail of a giant desert centipede is an adaptation to confuse predators. If a predator grabs the back end, the centipede can bite and retreat. The key is, the head has LONG AND SKINNY antennae, while the tail has thick, stout MODIFIED legs.

ANTENNAE

MODIFIED BACK LEGS

creature," I said, addressing the audience, "so let's do this: I'm going to take it out of this container so we can see its body segmentation and the little hooks on those feet. You ready for that?" *Easier said than done*, I thought. Turning the cube closer to me, I reached in with the forceps, just barely touching the centipede's back. *WHAP!* It didn't like that. In a flash, the creature reared its head around and struck at the tool in my hands.

"*Uwugh!*" I shuddered. "Yuck. Okay, maybe I need to pin down its head...." I set down the forceps and pointed my finger straight down above it, but right as I went to apply pressure...*WHAM!* It jumped up at me, and I jolted my hand back, barely missing a bite.

"Jeez! See how fast it is?" I cringed. "They're as speedy as they are dangerous. Man, there's just no good way to go about this." Determined to avoid those fangs, this time I lowered my whole hand in the capsule, thumb down, hovering over the centipede's head.

I took a deep breath and held it; then, with one swift motion, I pressed my thumb down and pinned the centipede's head on the floor of the cube. Immediately, I felt the creature twist and

Ouch, ouch, ouch!

turn, grabbing for anything within reach. Carefully, I slid my fingers around the sides of its head, getting a good hold on it, and cautiously raised the angry myriapod out of the clear box. Flailing its body about, the centipede finally found the skin on my hand with its legs and dug in.

"Ouch, ouch, ouch!" I winced. "Each one of these hooks is incredibly sharp!"

I could feel each muscle in its body working against me and was reminded of the strength these animals possess. Each segment of its body can move independently from the others, and between each, there's a joint that allows incredible flexibility.

"Wow!" I exclaimed. "The exoskeleton on this animal is rock solid. I can feel each leg pulling down, trying to get those fangs closer for a bite." Just as I said that, the centipede jerked its head down, opened its jawlike maxillipeds (those are the fangs I was talking about!), and tried to dig into my fingernail. *Good gravy!* My heart nearly leaped out of my chest as I quickly grasped it with my other hand before it found its target.

"Almost got me right there." I panicked, prying the biting creature back. "I do not have as good a hold as I thought. Wow, I can actually see venom coming out of the maxilliped, look at

that!" Clearly, this powerful centipede was in fighting mode and wanted to escape.

"I'm going to place it back into the container here and take a minute to compose myself before we get into the bite." I slid the bug cube across the table and lowered the centipede. When I let go, I snatched my hand out as fast as I could, leaving the creature to the confines of its container once more.

Pacing around the dry desert, I gathered my thoughts. When I think back to all the bites and stings, only one stands out as having been truly, catastrophically bad, and that was the Gila monster. After that, I promised myself two things: I'd never be bitten by a venomous snake, and I'd never take a bite from the giant desert centipede.

Well, there I was, on the precipice of breaking part of that promise. After all the comments asking for it, and all the stories I'd read about it, I had to know: What was the pain really like? *Remember what Wildman Phil said, Coyote, I* told myself. *It's worse than a rattlesnake bite.*

In the end, regardless of pain, it would come down to how my body reacted to the venom. Giant desert centipedes have a toxic concoction of hemotoxins, which destroy blood cells; neurotoxins, which attack nerves; and myotoxins, which affect muscles. Altogether, these components are what allow them to take down large prey items like ground squirrels and mice, as well as reptiles.

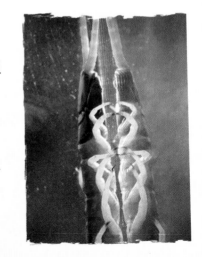

As the sun rose higher in the sky, I felt fear creeping up my neck and a nauseous sensation in my stomach as I walked back to the set. A lump of doubt grew heavy in my throat, but I crouched at the table. If nothing else, I was determined to prove that this myriapod means business, and if this was what it took to show the world that they should respect and steer clear of these creatures, it would be worth it.

"Well, this just became a reality." I gulped. Then I shifted the container closer, prepared to gently pin the creature and pick it up. With conviction, I swiftly pressed down, and the

Oh boy, this is it.

centipede snapped into action, flinging the rest of its body in a circle. Once its back end found my hand, it grappled on with its sharp legs.

"Ah! *Sssst!*" I said, wincing as I lifted it up to my face. "Those legs are really digging into me. Look at those fangs...." Squinting my eyes, I stared straight into the weaponry of the beast, noticing clear droplets of venom already forming at the tips of its fangs. It was primed and ready to bite. I shut my eyes, shook my head, and immediately turned my focus back to the cameras.

"Now, as always, I have an **epinephrine** pen," I stated, waving the medical device in the air. Epinephrine is an emergency medication used to reverse the effects of a severe allergic reaction. Although I don't typically need it for bites, I've had EpiPens on hand for every venomous insect sting I've ever intentionally taken.

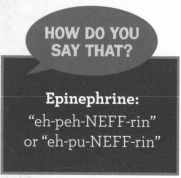

HOW DO YOU SAY THAT?

Epinephrine:
"eh-peh-NEFF-rin"
or "eh-pu-NEFF-rin"

"*Annnd,*" I said, gesturing toward the camera, "an emergency satellite phone."

"Never had to use it," Mark chimed in. "Please don't let today be the first time..."

With the centipede still grasped between my fingers, I lifted my left arm and set it across the table, palm up. As I focused on my breathing, I could feel a wave of anxiety

WOW!

Giant desert centipedes are ferocious predators and can subdue prey up to fifteen times their weight!

Here we go...

wash over me as my forehead flushed and beads of sweat trickled down my nose.

"Okay, here we go. Ready?" I looked at Mark, who gave a curt nod, then Mario, who returned a weak smile.

Okay, I repeated to myself. *Okay...here we go.* With one last breath, I started my intro. "I'm Coyote Peterson, and I'm about to be bitten by the giant...desert...centipede."

Flashes of heat washed over me as I started the countdown. After *one*, I hesitated, trying to clear the lump from my throat. At *two*, I draped the centipede's body on my arm. At *three*, I lowered its menacing head down onto my skin and held my breath. As soon as it was within reach of my arm, it cranked open its wide venomous daggers.

SHING! Like two searing hooks, I felt the giant desert centipede's fangs grasp a big chunk of my skin, then immediately—*FING!* It turned and pierced another. *TWO BITES!*

"*Aaaah! Aargh!*" I bellowed, quickly letting it drop

from my fingers. The centipede writhed around on
the table, then darted for escape, but I flipped the
container over on top of it, blocking its path, and then
I sprang to my feet.

"Ddrrrrruuuuuuuuuugh!" I was immediately bent
over, my right hand instinctively gripping my forearm
as tightly as possible as I felt the searing venom sprawl
out under my skin like a spider's web. *"Rrruuuargh!"*
I knelt back down, trying to point to the four red
impressions on my skin with my shaking hand.

"OH MY GOSH!" I screamed. "Right there's where
the fangs went in, do you see those puncture marks?"
I sputtered, barely able to speak through my clenched
jaw. I tried to sit still, but the adrenaline shooting
through my body wouldn't allow it. I tried to take
deep breaths, but my lungs felt tight as my heart
thundered in my chest. *BaDUMP baDUMP baDUMP!*

"FFFFFFtttttt!" I spat, crashing down on the
ground.

"Describe the pain!" Mark reminded me as I fell
over sideways on the sand.

"*Huuurrugh!* Immediately searing!" I growled. "This is so much worse than a bullet ant sting!" It was hard to put words together. I could only focus on the jarring, brutal blasts exploding in my limb as the venom ripped through my veins.

"This is the worst pain I have felt since the Gila monster." I seethed, shutting my eyes. I felt disoriented as alarming white spots flashed before my eyes. I gasped for air as I rolled back over and managed to get to my knees.

"I can see where they went in right there. Double chomp!" Mark said.

"Could you even see that?" I slurred. "It bit, curled the skin up, and then let go and bit a second time." Throughout the first few minutes, I went from kneeling to rolling on the ground to pacing to panting... but honestly, I barely remember any of it. I threw myself back down at the table when Mark spoke up:

"Talk to me. I gotta know you're not in serious trouble."

Okay, okay, I said to myself. *You can do this!*

"It's different than anything I've ever felt," I insisted. "It is absolutely searing, just...ARGH! *UURGH!*" I wanted so badly to keep talking, but my mind was frozen in shock. "I'm sorry, I can't compose words right now, man. Ugh! *Urrrgh!*"

My chest was heaving with every breath, and my eyes began to water. My mouth felt drier than the desert around us, so I reached for a bottle of water at my feet and desperately guzzled it down.

There was barely any blood at all. In fact, it didn't *look* like anything was wrong other than the small welts forming around the pinhole-size wounds. Underneath, however, it felt as though microscopic, white-hot razor blades were tearing through my flesh, and I could feel a tightness as my arm began to swell. Finally, feeling the wrath of the toxins creep up past my elbow, I thought of the only thing that might help.

"We might

I can feel the venom spreading up my arm.

need to use that venom extractor," I squawked. I had never felt so overwhelmed by a painful presentation or sting in my life. As much as I tried to hold it in, the anguish came

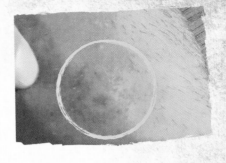

bursting from my throat with sprays of spit as I grunted, trying not to scream. My vision was blurry from the

water in my eyes, and I clenched my shaking fists. I was beginning to regret this intentional bite as I squeezed my eyes shut in a tight grimace and spat, "Just cut the cameras! We gotta get this venom out of my arm!"

Venom extractors are controversial. There is little evidence that they work, and they are never recommended for serious venomous bites. In this situation, however, I was desperate. We had never used an extractor on bites or stings before, but because of the location and intensity, it seemed like the only thing that might help. Once all the pieces were in place, we resumed filming.

"Let's use the tourniquet," I sputtered. "I just want to...so it can...*ooh*. I think I'm gonna vomit." Typically, tourniquets are used to limit blood flow, but in this instance, I was hoping it would slow the spread of venom.

It's important to note that the rubber tourniquet was only lightly placed on my arm. You never want to secure one too tightly because it forces your heart to beat faster and prevents vital circulation to your skin and muscles.

"All right, guys," I said shakily. "I'm going to try and see if we can't suck some of that venom out of my forearm. The pain is so bad I'm almost in tears." As Mark wiped any remaining venom or bacteria from my skin with an alcohol pad, I could see the welts had already expanded in size. Since the bite marks were pretty close together, Mark placed the cup of the device over all four at once. *FUMP!* As Mark pulled up on the extractor's main lever, my skin suctioned into the containment capsule and rose up like a mound inside the plastic.

"*Awwrrgh!*" I bellowed. Mark turned the top, locking it into place, and slowly but surely, blood-tinged yellow droplets rose to the surface of my skin. "Gah! That's only making it hurt worse!"

"Tell us if you feel like we need to get you out of here," Mario insisted. I nodded, unable to speak. The agony continued to build and wash over me as I thought, *Enough is enough...get it off!*

"Okay, unlock it," I said, trying to fiddle with the handle. Mark put down his camera and grabbed the extractor. Disengaging the suction, he twisted it free with a *CLICK*, releasing the

pressure and allowing him to pull it away. "Ah! *Ssst!* Ugh!" Each bite mark was capped with beads of fluid, and the circular imprint where the forced suction of the cup had been was throbbing.

"You see how black and blue it's already turning?" I asked through growling gasps. "This absolutely eclipses any insect sting I have ever taken. It makes the bullet ant feel like a bee sting. In this moment, I am regretting getting bitten by the giant desert centipede, guys."

I wiped the fluid away with another alcohol swab and actually tried the venom extractor a second time with the same results: waves of scalding pain. After leaving it on for a few minutes, I had to throw in the towel. Truth be told, I don't know if the venom extractor made the bite worse, but it definitely didn't make it better.

By now, the desert sun was scorching hot, making my delirious daze feel like an inferno. I was physically and mentally exhausted and wanted nothing more than delightful air-conditioning, an ice pack, and a couch.

From Phil's terrifying story, I'd known that the venom of the giant desert centipede would be excruciating. Like with Gila monster venom, the pain was debilitating and built in intensity over time. What I didn't know was just how long it would last. After filming was done, I feverishly washed and rinsed my arm under a cold tap, feeling only a second of relief before—*BOOM!* Another wave of increased pain hit me like a massive ton of bricks.

DID YOU KNOW?

When they hatch, young giant desert centipedes are called nymphs and only start out with about ten legs. When they grow, they shed their exoskeletons and gain up to eighteen more legs after each molt!

I tried sitting on the couch, but the squirming of my body forced me back up. Mark, Mario, and I tried to do everyday, normal things, like get lunch and go shopping, but I was in such discomfort the entire time, I couldn't function. Hour after hour, the pain increased until finally, by three o'clock in the afternoon, it reached its zenith.

My arm continued to swell and was now over twice its normal size, and it felt like a bomb had exploded under my skin. It was like a gaping wound that you couldn't see. I could feel the venom aggressively attacking my blood cells, seeping through and exploding from the inside out, which was very different from any of the stings I'd taken.

I tried, with every fiber of my being, to tough through it, but after another couple of hours, the pain was unrelenting. *Is it ever going to stop?* I pleaded. *I think I need help!* Exhausted and defeated, I asked Mario to take me to the hospital, something I had never done after intentional bites or stings of the past.

The emergency room was, in all honestly, the best call I could possibly have made. When my friend Wildman Phil warned me about the giant desert centipede's bite, he told me I'd have to go, and he was right. Provided with strong anti-inflammatory medication and something mild to manage pain, the following thirty-six hours were much more bearable.

I know what you're thinking: *Thirty-six hours?!* Yes, that is how long it lasted. The swelling remained for about four days, and the holes closed after a week. Still, it wasn't over. Little, hard BB-like welts formed under my skin and itched severely for over a month after the bite.

So, what did I learn from the bite of this fearsome creature? That my fears were warranted!

When you compare the alien-like nature, venomous bite, and huge size of the giant desert centipede to

other creepy-crawlies of the United States, nothing measures up. Their unbelievable speed propels them through the desert, and their hooked legs give them the ability to grip on to and climb almost any surface. Combined with the catastrophic pain induced by their bite, there's no question....This animal is truly a living nightmare!

If you're ever venturing out in the southwestern United States, be on your guard. It's not just snakes, scorpions, and Gila monsters you should avoid while hiking in the desert. Potentially dangerous animals like the giant desert centipede share the environment with these other venomous species and are a lot more common than you think. I present little-known creatures to you, the Coyote Pack, so that you can learn about them and their defense mechanisms, and how to avoid a painful interaction. While I would never encourage you to be afraid for no reason, it's okay to be afraid of something when you know how dangerous it could be. The giant desert centipede is one formidable foe that, in my opinion, warrants fear and a healthy level of respect. This is definitely an animal who I avoid interactions with and would never be bitten by again. The risk of facing that pain just isn't worth it.

I am almost certain that each and every one of you has seen this episode, and before I sign off, I know the *real* question you want the answer to: *Did Coyote Peterson cry from the bite of the giant desert centipede?* Well, for the first time in my adult life, the pain from that creature's bite was so intense that it caused my eyes to water. Does that count as crying? I'll leave it up to you to decide!

THAT'S A WRAP!

My main goal and mission for every wildlife encounter is always education. I want to shed light on these amazing and misunderstood creatures, prove that they don't go out of their way to bite humans, and hopefully turn your sense fear into respect. To achieve that, the Brave Wilderness team and I knew that it would take something a little *wilder* than just presenting these animals in simple videos.

Whether they're snapping turtles or snakes, crustaceans or canines, each of these animals is a valuable, important part of our world, and fascinating in their own way. If I can teach you something about these little-known and often reclusive beasts that is fun, easy to understand, and utterly unforgettable, then I have properly done my job.

I'm the luckiest guy on the planet. I get to travel to unique locations, have wild adventures, see and interact with animals in their natural environments... and then I get to share these stories with you, the Coyote Pack. Each and every one of you is the reason I do what I do.

So, **thank you** for reading my books, for watching our shows, and most important, for loving the world of animals and adventure just as much—if not more—than I do!

Be Brave...Stay Wild—we'll see ya on the next adventure!